APPETITE FOR DESIGN

EAT ME

PRODUCT · PACKAGING · ART · BRANDING · INTERIOR

APPETITE FOR DESIGN

EAT ME

PRODUCT · PACKAGING · ART · BRANDING · INTERIOR

Published and distributed by
viction:workshop ltd.

viction:ary™

viction:workshop ltd.
Unit C, 7/F, Seabright Plaza, 9-23 Shell Street,
North Point, Hong Kong
Url: www.victionary.com   Email: we@victionary.com
 www.facebook.com/victionworkshop
 www.twitter.com/victionary_
 www.weibo.com/victionary

Edited and produced by viction:workshop ltd.

Concepts & art direction by Victor Cheung
Book design by viction:workshop ltd.

Second Edition
ISBN 978-988-19438-5-9
Printed and bound in China

MENU

———

A GREAT START
004–007

CREATIVE SPECIALS
008–249

PASSION AND CREATIVE IDEAS SERVED IN ART CREATIONS,
SOCIAL EVENTS, BRANDING, PACKAGING, INTERIOR AND OTHER
PRODUCTS INSPIRED BY FOOD AND HOW WE LIKE TO EAT

TALK TO INSIDERS

FIVE ARTISTS & DESIGNERS EXPAND ON THEIR URGE TO CREATE
WITH FEATURES OF LOCAL FOOD CULTURE ON THE SIDE

A FINE FINISH
250–255

BIOGRAPHIES OF 87 ARTISTS & DESIGNERS
FROM AROUND THE WORLD

ACKNOWLEDGEMENTS
256

FOREWORD

Katrin Oeding
Creative Director
KOREFE

People eat in the most different ways. Sometimes it has to be fast, other times it cannot take long enough. One eats alone from a plastic table, romantically in pairs in a restaurant or you celebrate a feast in a big circle. A meal can be frozen, cold, luke warm, warm, hot. It comes in several courses or just as one whole portion. One can order food, have it cooked or be the one himself to be standing in the kitchen.

Meat eater, vegetarians, vegans and fruitarians fight for the moral conduct to follow. One eats with the fingers, with chopsticks, with knife and fork or spoon, simply from cardboard or elegantly from porcelain. Countries are proud of their traditional dishes which have not changed for centuries. On the other side all over the world people keep trying out new recipes.

That variety exhibits a tremendous potential for creative expansion. It already starts with purchasing the right ingredients. The options of packaging a product have exploded over the last years. In contrary to simple tins in earlier years, new methods for conservation as well as eating habits have led to a great miscellaneousness of packaging forms. An example of a design aiming to adapt to the changing claims of modern working life are packages that function as plate and cutlery at the same time in order to pay in the constant lack of time. But not only the forms have changed, also the variety of materials available has increased. Furthermore a unique design of the packaging layout is getting more and more important for communicational means. Nowadays it is advertised and elucidated on packaging, with recipe suggestions placed next to company stories.

Once the ingredients are bought, the creative preparation starts. One of the most interesting forms is the molecular gastronomy. Comestibles with explicitly new characteristics are developed by using scientific results of chemical and physical kind. A good example is Ferran Adrià's "melon caviar". The tastes we are used to are consciously confounded in

order to strengthen our flavour perceptions. This disruption makes the barriers to art in a state of flux. Hence, as the first cook ever Adriàs was even invited to join in at the documenta 12 in Kassel a few years ago. Speaking of arts, ingestion has been one of its favourite topics for centuries. Warhol's Campbell soup cans are a prominent example, or Ferreri's famous movie, *La Grande Bouffe* (1973). And there is no evidence this topic might ever run dry.

However, each extraordinary meal is supposed to be eaten up at some point, as this is what it was made for in the first place. But nowadays humankind are not satisfied with a table in cloth anymore. Not only is the food supposed to be an event, but also the atmosphere. Therefore interior decorators and designers of tableware have become nearly as important as the chefs themselves. The concept of the illy-Pop-Up café gives a hint of the future when it scrutinised the idea of a long-established gastronomy by popping up all over the place and only for short periods of time.

This book gives an idea of where this development leads us. *EAT ME* gives a fantastic overview on food as a cultural phenomenon. Find inspiration, maybe while having your favourite dish. Because although the history of food is an old one: it is long not over and always needs fresh minds with astonishing ideas.

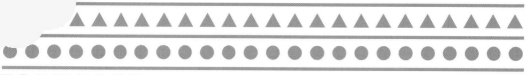

FOREWORD

Sylvain Allard
Graphic Design Professor
UQAM

Archaeologists have often been retracing the lifestyles of ancient civilisations by analysing food remains and culinary artefacts. In fact, the study of dishes and utensils can be helpful for understanding ancient manners and customs in order to trace the history of civilisations that precede us. The relation between man and food is a fascinating evolution process. First as hunter-gatherers, then as farmer-ranchers and finally as traders, man therefore was able to exploit the food that was nearby and immediately available and transform it with tools they had created for that purpose.

Obviously, food is a basic and vital need. It is common to all living beings. But besides the physiological need for sustenance lies the desire of those whose objective is the absolute pleasure of eating. Desire is distinctive to each individual and culture, which all have their specific codes and references. What looks like a feast to some people could be unappealing to others and vice versa. The enjoyment of food is essentially a multi-sensory experience. It consists of a series of visual, olfactory and taste stimuli, which interact with each other until satiety is reached. Socially, the meal divides the day in downtime, which also promote human interaction. It is a time for rituals, decorum and propriety specific to family gatherings, social, cultural and religious ceremonials.

While in the past, food was closely bound to Mother Nature's generosity, the last century has seen a complete shift as food industrialisation, transportation and packaging have made global food culture possible. These elements have contributed, in a relatively short time, to a boom in global food culture allowing the consumer to enjoy easy access to any food anywhere in the world all year round. Today, people eat sushi in Milan, drink champagne in Mexico City and savour maple syrup in Tokyo. There are no more boundaries to food culture. On the other hand, many questions remain about the future of world food culture. Is food globalisation a benefit or a hazard? Should we fear cultural uniformity and thus the loss of specific regional uniqueness or should we welcome the birth of a new planetary culture? Will the future preserve the richness and diversity of world cuisine or will it become homogenous and monotonous? By mixing food cultures as we do, aren't we playing a trick on the archaeologists of the future?

Since ever, food was strictly a cultural matter but traditional comforting rituals are now giving space to the excitement of novelty either imported from other cultures or simply introduced by new brands. This fascination with novelty is a key element in the development

of new food products. The competition is fierce on the shelf and brands have very little time to make their appeal before being replaced by other new ones. In the current market, global brands transcend local values and are dictating new rituals. Food culture freed from strict national references, take freely mixing genres and pave the way for experimental cuisine whose sources of inspiration are diverse and from all over the world.

Today, the art of the table, like other artistic expressions, is more transversal than ever. Food is an endless source of inspiration. It implies many design fields. Stores, packages, dishes and food shape itself are no longer perceived as strictly functional elements but as part of the overall food experience. New technologies and new materials also promote the emergence of innovative approaches to food preparation and presentation. The boundaries between science, art and tradition are disappearing to give way to more experimental and surprising cuisines.

Who said to stop to play with our food anyway? Why not enlarging the experience to trigger all other senses by building a playful story around the brand. After all, food is a source of joy and why not including fun in all the aspects around it. If brands aim at being distinctive, shouldn't they propose a bit of happening in their products? If food has been, for a long time, perceived as a very serious matter, what we see more and more today is the free introduction of humour in food culture. Borrowing visual aesthetic codes from other sectors [where] designers today are proposing new stories and rituals transforming humdrum meals into fun and exciting experiences.

This book celebrates the festive food and the importance of its place in our lives. It is an overview of the creativity and innovation in the service of a basic need — eating. It certainly talks about what we eat, but above all how important this basic act has transformed through our traditions and rituals in progress. It is the insatiable and infinite search for new and innovative food ideas that transform the basic need of eating into an art of living.

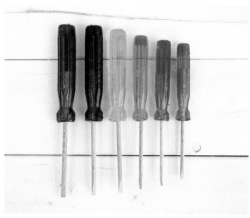

LOLLY TOOLS
Korefe

The Deli Garage is a food and beverage label that sells handmade delicatessen foods with the design and functionality of products commonly found in garages. By reversing the regular lollipop form, screwdrivers are turned into fruity lollipops in a classic white leather tool bag.

SOSO
Eduardo del Fraile

Available in eight colours, these plastic eggs combine packaging with practicality as refillable shakers and cellars for SOSO Factory's salt products, seasoned with spice and herb to match different dishes. The colours offer an easy taste reference for chefs from the crowded delicatessen shelves.

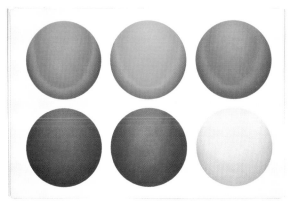

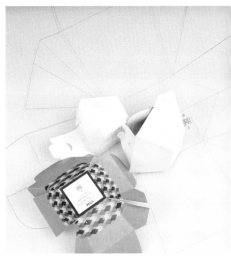

DAO CHA
PEGA D&E

Dao refers to the gesture of pouring and the act of telling in Chinese. Containing a tea bag, water-tight teapot and tea cup in one slim design, *Dao Cha* celebrates tea traditions with convenience and sophistication at once. The teapot is folded from one single sheet resistant to heat and weight.

POLAR ICE
Atsuhiro Hayashi

Manufacture / monos

Amidst the outcry of environmental awareness, these ice moulds are designed to remind you of the critical situation at the two poles whenever you use these ice blocks and see the polar bear or penguins slowly melt into your drink.

Design / John Lumbus
Photo / Jon Stanley Austin

STORM IN A TEA CUP
Laikingland

A literal homage to the idiom "A storm in a teacup", this kinetic art pieces render an angry sea tossing its traveller under a shining bolt of lightning as you turn its handle on the side. Both Royal Delft (blue) and New English (white) are available at Tate Galleries in London and Moss in New York.

VODKA
Korefe

Named 'POWERFUEL', Deli Garage's vodka offers flavours of natural fresh fruit mixed with herb, such as melon with mint and ginger with coriander, as well as blackberry with espresso. Robust giants compatible to the flavours are silkscreened on the flasks to cater a hip and extraordinary taste.

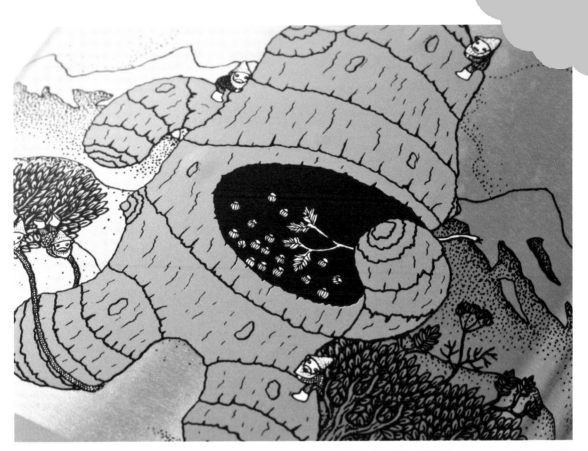

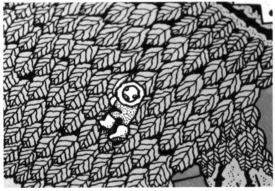

STACKED CUPS
the.

With its idea rooted in the cups that keep piling up in the sink after parties, the. created these
cups that naturally nestle within each other as one porcelain cup. *Stacked Cups* come in as
triple and double cups, plus the single ones to be built up to almost a feet high.

SNAP AND DINE

Demelza Hill

Snap and Dine is a single-use three-course table setting that marries fine dining formality with pick-and-go convenience. Its objective to heighten outdoor dining experience is achieved through its visual references to ceramics and the kiss-cuttings to detach the cutlery in a snap.

MAKE A WISH RING
Bettina Nissen Design

Candle holders might as well be a keepsake for special days. *Make A Wish* is a redesign of the little iconic device, using rapid prototyping to configure the holder's bottom part into a ring. The rings are currently available in five materials and colour options in four sizes.

ICE-CREAMS
Après Ski

Celebrating the Bauhaus spirit, the fauna and flora of nature and the universe, these ice-cream pendants reinterpret shapes and patterns of found materials to make a unique piece. Featured here are *The Last Ice-creams of the Summer* and *Constellation* from the collection.

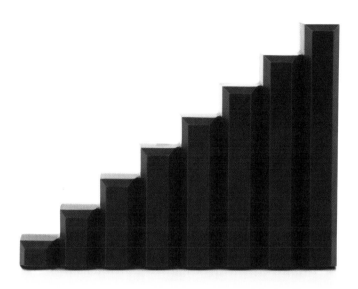

THE MOST HONEST CHOCOLATE TABLET
5.5 Designers

Chocolate is a great delight that is hard to resist. Called *The Most Honest Chocolate Tablet*, this box makes energy content explicit with caloric values for respective bars specified on its front. A perfect measure for sweet addicts to conduct oneself while savouring Chocolate Factory treats.

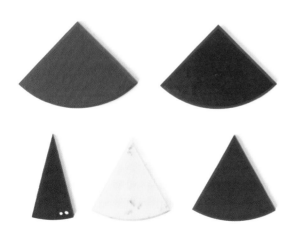

THE GÂTEAU

THE GÂTEAU
5.5 Designers

Choosing a cake to quench all guests is always a difficult task, but chocolate desserts are always a guarantee. Gathering six chocolate flavours in different portions, *The Gâteau* allows Chocolate Factory to consider all possibilities to mix and match chocolate to consumers' taste.

THE INTROVERTED
5.5 Designers

A series of chocolate domes are cast in proportion to their cocoa content. With one housing another, these lids is cast to imagine a true trip into chocolate's heart, the ultimate taste of cocoa with a cocoa bean at its heart. *The Introverted* is yet another project produced for Chocolate Factory.

PARAPHRASE
Carl Kleiner & Evelina Kleiner

Using food substances as the sole ingredient for its tonal palette, the series is the paraphrase of
famous minimalist paintings, sculptors and their original compositions inspired by minimalism. Materials adopted include coffee powder, curry powder, wild rice and root crops.

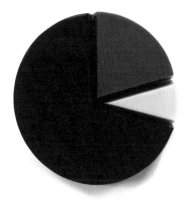

CHOCOLATE EDITIONS
Chocolate Editions by Mary & Matt

Chocolate Editions celebrates candy bar as a perfect pop object. Originally made as gifts for friends and family, the chocolates quickly grows into a full confection line. Its inspirations are mainly Mary & Matt's personal favourites, such as the artworks by Sol LeWitt and David Hockney.

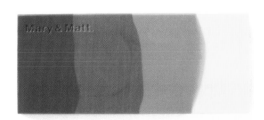

MOONCAKE GIFT PACK
Point-Blank Design Ltd.

With its origin in the Chinese agricultural society, the Moon Festival is where Chinese gather and share food to celebrate prosperity and cultural richness. Incorporating a poetic picture of this point of time, auspicious phrases are custom-illustrated on the mooncake gift box to heighten the joy.

DESIGNER BARBECUE THE PARTNERS 8/7/11 6:30PM   DESIGNER BARBECUE THE PARTNERS 8/7/11 6:30PM

BURN BABY BURN
The Partners

The Partners was planning on hosting their annual summer barbecue. Making it official, The Partners took on the barbecue itself to create these posters to call on friends and family to enjoy beers and burgers. All items featured in the posters were physically burnt on a barbecue for real.

DESIGNER BARBECUE THE PARTNERS 8/7/11 6:30PM

DESIGNER BARBECUE THE PARTNERS 8/7/11 6:30PM

DESIGNER BARBECUE THE PARTNERS 8/7/11 6:30PM

DESIGNER BARBECUE THE PARTNERS 8/7/11 6:30PM

FABFOOD
Linus Morales

Depicting a heap of typical Swedish fast food modelled into or stamped with luxury fashion
brands, Fabfood originated as a poster series to set off a chic restaurant in Swedish boutique
hotel. The collection was meant to be a little provocative but visually graphic and clean as pop art.

1

2

ART ON ZARB
Zarb Champagne

Zarb has initiated an art project where artists are summoned to reinterpret Zarb's champagne bottles for communication and exhibition tours. Participants include Aarsman & Sola, Deux d'Amsterdam, Dieuwertje, Vin Burnham, Zena Holloway and Miktor & Molf.

1 / Fire-extinguisher by Zarb
2 / Super Soaker by EdhV
3 / Rocket Launch Platform by La Bolleur
4 / Bones by Cedric Lacquieze
5 / Flowers by Cedric Lacquieze
6 / Feathers by Zarb
7 / Fragile by Zarb
8 / Golf by Zarb

3

4

5

6

7

8

SWEET MEAT
Jasmin Schuller || Visual Entertainment

Digital Art Direction / TH32TY TWO
Asistant / Katharina Oberegger

Unlike the usual dessert recipes, *Sweet Meat* is in fact a dessert menu made from real meal and blood requiring extra effort and attention to achieve its delicately 'sweet' look. The series is meant to be thought-provoking towards meat consumption than just a feast for the eyes.

BRICKSTONES
Korefe

Continuing on its theme on garage items, The Deli Garage's easy bakery kits allow homemade sponge cakes to wall up to serve. Developed together with a small mill in Northern Germany, the package includes six "brick moulds" and formulated cake mix in mini "cement bags".

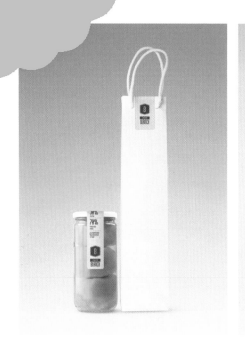

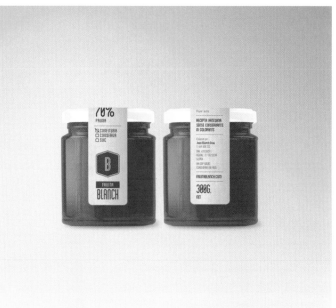

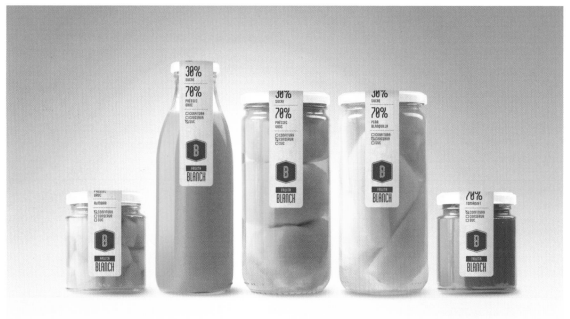

FRUITA BLANCH
Atipus

Fruita Blanch, a family business with a long tradition, introduced their low-sugar, chemical-free preserved products. Labels of different sizes are designed to emphasise the brand's tradition, artisan methods and the deepest care in what they do.

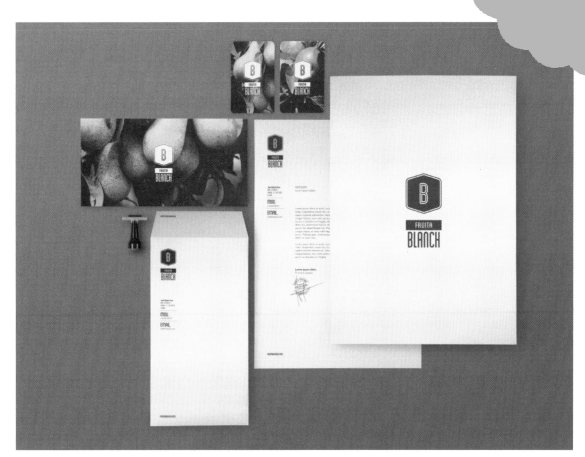

RECEPTA ARTESANA
SENSE CONSERVANTS NI COLORANTS

100% NATURAL
PRÉSSEC GROC I SUCRE

BLANCH

BLANCH CAPS

ABCDEFGHIJKLMNOPQRSTUVWXYZ

BLANCH CONDENSED

ABCDEFGHIJKLMNOPQRSTUVWXYZ
0123456789 0%Ç.:

LH2O
Pedrita

Graphics / Marco Balesteros
Copywriting / Frederico Duarte
Photo / Tiago Pinto

LH2O defines water as a new 'form' of sustenance rather than just an element. The faceted bottle seeks to illustrate the purity of Luso natural mineral water by letting in more light while optimising storage space and its function to minimise damage during transportation and on the rack.

AGUA+
Method

Aqua+ was an exploratory exercise for a startup food and beverage company stressing
sustainability. Using ecofriendly plastics as the core material, the container was interned to
reduce the overall use and waste of materials throughout the production process.

OHMINE
Ohmine Shuzou Co., Ltd

Design / Stockholm Design Lab

Ohmine sake comes in three qualities, decided by the percentage of original rice grain used for brewing the sake. The lesser the better. Translating the idea onto its packaging, the sake bottles and glasses impart its designation in the silhouette of rice grains that talks to the world.

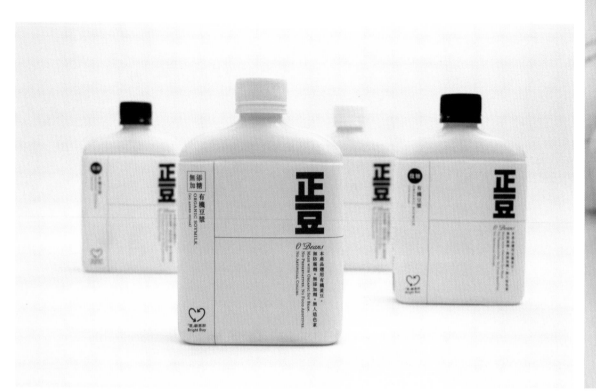

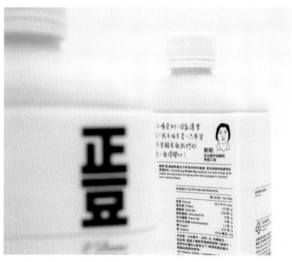

O'BEANS
CoDesign Ltd

O'bean is a soy drink line launched in support of mental patients' readaptation to social life, and part of the scheme includes reusing the beverage bottles for a community soap production programme. A minimal amount of materials and graphics was proposed to cope with the theme.

BEFORE

AFTER

MLK ORGANIC DAIRY
Depot WPF

Mlk's milk line was among its first organic diary products to tap into the consumer market. Stressing 'naturalness' in its product, different corners of the farm are depicted to give a subtle hint of its natural source. Pencil sketches are alluded to its manual labour involved in its production.

mlk

low fat milk
0.5%

organic dairy

mlk

mild
yoghurt
5.5%

organic dairy

mlk

full
cream
milk
10%

organic dairy

mlk
15% sour cream

organic dairy

mlk

THE SUPERNATURAL
Inhouse Design

Brewed with organic grapes sourced from the winery's hillside estate in New Zealand, the Supernatural is exclusively introduced to the American market. Its sustainable qualities was conveyed in its name as well as the label with a juxtaposition of images to indicate its craftsmanship.

TAPAS WINE
Eduardo del Fraile

Tapas Wine is a good Spanish wine exported at an affordable price. The graphical solution has taken reference from Spanish classics, ranging from handwrittem bar menuson the walls and waiters' shouting across the room. The little wooden sticks are what patrons would use to clean their teeth.

RIVIERA DESSERTS
Nelson Associates

Photo / John Ross
Photo Retouching / Gianluca Fearn-Paoli

Riviera's sundae flavours are beautifully illustrated in three stunning shots, with sundae sauce slowly dripping off invisible lemon and candies to tempt on each pack. The avant-garde approach is aimed to take the dessert to public attention at upscale supermarkets across the UK.

KLEIN CONSTANTIA HONEY
At Pace

Hidden amongst the gum trees of wine estate Klein Constantia are some beehives full of buzzing insects, hard at work. Rather as a charming consumer gift than for commercial gain, the packaging puts the hectic scene into pictures, in company with a few bees to escort their precious honey.

Christmas Tea*

Otkrij čaroliju Božića ispod
sniježnog pokrivača i podijeli je
sa voljenom osobom.

CHRISTMAS TEA
Mint

Sharing is the essence of Christmas. Considering the number of Christmas trees being disposed
after the holidays, Christmas Tea comes as fir trees that can be shared and fit in small households
such as student dorms. Christmas Tea is a sustainable design entirely made from natural materials.

—

▲▲▲▲▲▲▲▲▲▲▲▲▲▲▲▲▲▲▲▲▲▲▲▲▲▲▲▲▲▲▲

SAVVY STUDIO
FROM PICTOGRAMS TO BRAND STORIES
• 066–077 •

—

ESZTER IMRE
FROM MANUFACTURE TO DESIGN
• 078–087 •

▼▼▼▼▼▼▼▼▼▼▼▼▼▼▼▼▼▼▼▼▼▼▼▼▼▼▼▼▼▼

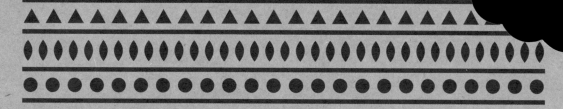

FROM PICTOGRAMS TO BRAND STORIES

Savvy Studio savvys what make culinary and brand experience a whole

HOW WOULD YOU REGARD FOOD AND ITS RELATIONSHIP TO MANKIND?

Food is one of the most important things for humanity. It's fuel for life. It helps define who you are and who you want to be.

HOW WOULD BRAND IDENTITY HELP TO ENHANCE THIS RELATIONSHIP?

A restaurant's identity is a shortcut from the chef's gastronomic proposal to the consumer. It is an opportunity to channel certain images and other sensations, and let people experience what you offer as a restaurant.

WHAT IS BRAND EXPERIENCE ABOUT? WHAT MAKE(S) EFFECTIVE BRANDING NOWADAYS?

Nowadays branding strategies can be very effective because we designers are not only creating just logos or pretty images, but also telling stories in a way. We design a language that becomes an experience for the consumer, and has an effect on people's life.

WHAT IS FOOD CULTURE IN MEXICO LIKE? WHAT SHOULD A FOREIGNER LOOK FOR IF THEY VISIT YOUR COUNTRY ONE DAY?

Mexican culture is eclectic, and people are friendly and always open to trying new things in every field. Since forever people have created dishes composed with more than 25 ingredients, and the result sometimes looks simpler than it actually is. You have to experiment to find new ways to enjoy food.

Inspiration can come when you are tasting great food. There are a lot of great restaurants in our country, of different styles. You can find a very traditional Mexican restaurant where you can try mole, or you can eat some great steaks, or find really fresh seafood cooked in interesting ways.

HOW DO YOU THINK FOOD CULTURE TODAY HAS REFASHIONED CREATIVE APPROACHES TO BRANDING STRATEGIES?

Today, what you eat can be a statement on your personality. The restaurants you visit and the food you make at home define an important aspect of your character. Branding and identity work in the very same way, you try to talk to a target and you expect them to identify with the brand.

▲▲▲▲▲▲▲▲▲▲▲▲▲▲▲▲▲▲▲▲▲▲▲▲▲▲

WHAT SEEMS TO BE THE NEW DIRECTIONS IN CREATING A STRATEGIC RESTAURANT DESIGN TODAY?

The whole experience — that is where things are going which make things memorable. It's not just the food. It's the way you invite people to your restaurant. Everything has to be consistently clever — the interior decoration, the waiters' uniform, the visual language of the place, the waiters' attitude, and of course, the menu itself.

People perceive the quality or the amount of creativity of your food from every angle.

HOW DO YOU NORMALLY START WITH A NEW PROJECT? WHAT ARE THE NECESSARY STEPS TO TAKE TO PERFECT YOUR DESIGNS?

We start by trying to get all the information from our client before we get down to design. We develop the brand and look for references, and do so until the whole concept and the brand's individual truth have been narrowed down.

Within the process of conceptualising the brand, we decide what kind of techniques and aesthetic the project might need, and whether it will need the fork of an illustrator or custom type designer, etc...

THE VIBRANCY OF NIGHT-LIFE IN TOKYO PREVAILS TOROTORO'S ADS AND IDENTITY. HOW DO THESE VISUALS COMPLETE TOROTORO'S VISION AND PATRONS' EXPECTATIONS FOR DINING AT TOROTORO?

This project in specific was a bit different because the menu was a fusion of Japanese and Mexican food. That's why we chose that name — 'Toro' as the fish and 'Toro' as the bull.

The styling for Japanese restaurants in Monterrey tend to be a cliché. Instead of going for the typical Japanese restaurant aesthetic in Mexico, the concept was based around the idea of [setting up] a restaurant in Tokyo. Departing from that concept, we found the freedom to create a dialogue between the two cultures.

The dining experience in the restaurant is really solid. It has a whole wall of flat screen LED TVs that show

Japanese-themed videos that we produced, and in a way this enormous screen transports you to Japan.

What you see in the restaurant's identity or the ads is what you get as soon as you walk into the restaurant.

WHAT KIND OF NEW ELEMENTS DO YOU WISH TO BRING INTO YOUR FUTURE BRANDING PROJECTS, AND WHY?

Infographics and a sustainable approach to every brand, consciousness about the present and the relationship between all of us and the environment we all live in. A sense of permanent building, a brand that can actually grow with time and become a more interesting and solid brand.

IS THERE SOMETHING ABOUT FOOD OR THE FOOD CULTURE THAT YOU WOULD BE EAGERLY EXPECTING TO SEE OR TASTE?

A more sustainable and natural way to eat without sacrificing the creativity of cooking.

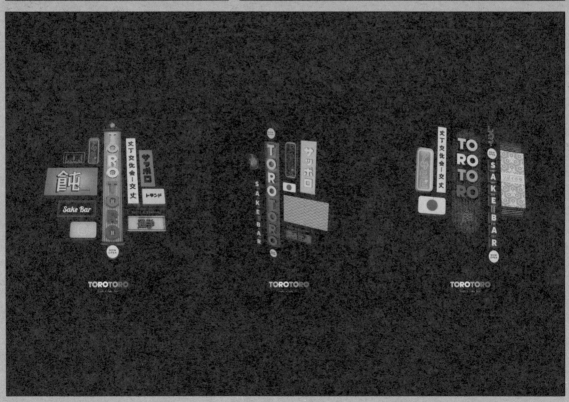

TOROTORO (2011) - Branding and visual identity to bring authentic Tokyo culture into TOROTORO, a Japanese restaurant in Monterrey, Mexico.

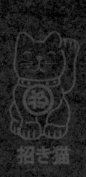

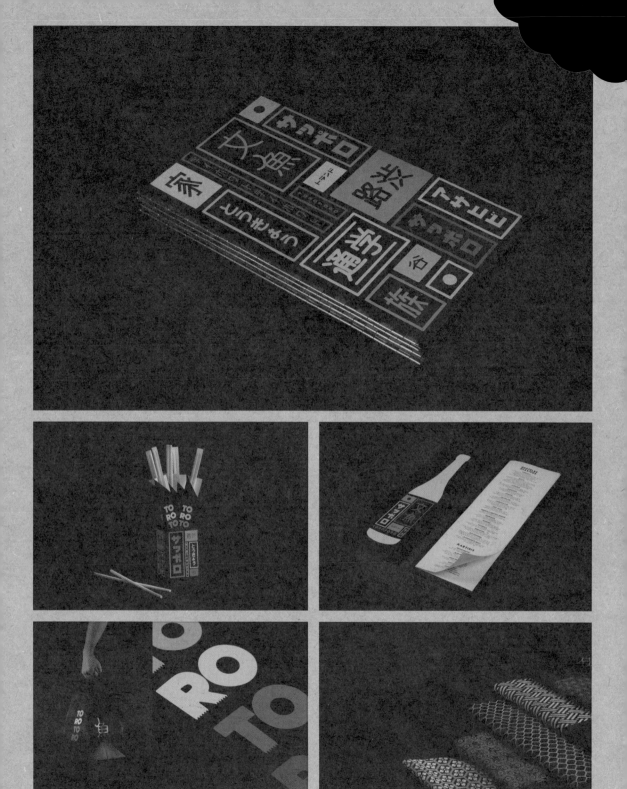

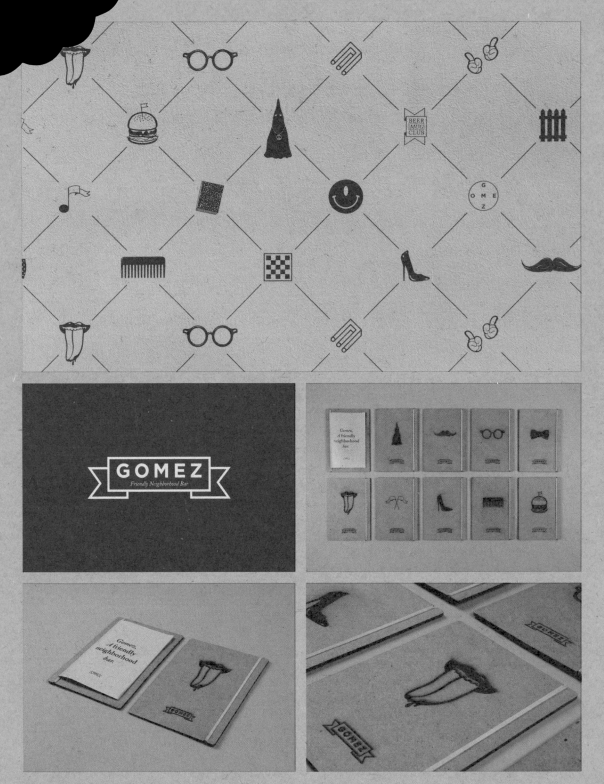

Gomez (2010) – Identity founded on amiability and a fun personality to correspond to the bar's neighbourhood in San Pedro Garza García, Mexico.

After-Office
Friendly.

the **Friendly** *Neighborhood Bar*

Gómez Morín

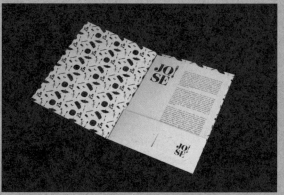

José Leos (2010) - Identity highlighting delicacy and efficiency that characterise
Chef José Leos' professionalism as a caterer in San Luis Potosí, Mexico.

Costa Chica (2011) - Identity and advertising stressing practicality and freshness of Costa Chica's seafood menu, similar to its sister restaurant, Costa Nueva, from the Mexican Pacific coast.

Villa De Patos (2010) - Branding to embrace the traditions and authenticity of Villa de Patos and their organic products for sale in supermarkets and their own store.

FROM MANUFACTURE TO DESIGN

Eszter Imre defines and refines the moments with a sensual grip

Portrait / Kata Kis

HOW WOULD YOU REGARD FOOD AND ITS RELATIONSHIP TO MANKIND? HOW DO YOU LIKE TO ENJOY FOOD?

Normal relationship to food is when we eat to satisfy our hunger and senses in a personal way. Some has developed a very strange relationship to food. Unfortunately eating disorders are a very frequent problem that should be more considered nowadays. Some try to use eating as a habit to satisfy needs of other kind, to feel safer, to satisfy the craving for love, or other psychic compulsion at the expense of health.

For me, my relation [to food] is personal. I give attention to what I let into my body as it is the closest physical relationship possible. Food is always about sharing and company. Whether it's in the company of many friends or that certain special person. Food, like all other pleasures of life, is best when shared. As eating is one of the great equalisers, we all need to do it regardless of social or professional status. We must eat, we can choose when and how we do it. We can decide on its circumstances that make it into an enjoyable activity.

On the other hand, eating is a ritual. [It concerns] the preparation of food. Eating gives us time for reflection. I like to take my time in both preparing and eating. When I prepare my breakfast I like to focus on every movement, to think about my day, prepare, plan. Breakfast lets me slowly sink into my day. I like eating when it brings

back memories. Rediscovering forgotten tastes of our childhood. Brings us home. But it's not only the taste, it's also about the smell, the sound and the look. If food is a combination of tastes, eating is a combination of senses. I want to add to this experience in my designs. Naturally I feel the experience is best if it is shared so a lot of focus in my work is about creating shared experiences. For me all circumstances are very important, the space, the bowl, the spoon... they all are part of the play.

WHAT ROLES DO UTENSILS AND TABLEWARE PLAY IN MODERN KITCHENS AND ON DINING TABLES TODAY?

I feel it's much more than being efficient tools. There are the basic shapes and functions and they are, as eating itself, universal in many ways. The kitchen is where everything happens. It is the heart of a home, a place we all can relate to. The basics are the same everywhere. So here lies the need for universality and the opportunity for personal expression. Combining these two is a challenge, but it's one worth taking on.

To be invited to a home for lunch or dinner is a great honour. You can invite others to your world through the food you make and the way you serve it. It says so much about you. The way we present the food we eat and the tools we use is a way of showing who we are. A gift is not about the paper it is wrapped in or the way it is wrapped, but it can tell a lot about who the giver is and their relationship with the receiver. I feel the same can be said about the relationship between food and the eater. The host and their guests. The utensils and tableware are tools, but also a medium for respect and personal style. Most other tools are created to cater professional needs we use to achieve other things. Designs for kitchen is designing for the ones who eat, i.e. everyone. It's for humans, pure and simple.

WHAT IS FOOD CULTURE LIKE IN HUNGARY? WHAT SHOULD A FOREIGNER LOOK FOR IF THEY VISIT YOUR COUNTRY ONE DAY?

The kitchen is, and always have been the centre of a home. When you step into a home you step into the kitchen, you step into the centre of life.

The fundamental difference from most European gastronomy is that the ancient Hungarian kitchen is often described as "pentatonic flavours harmony", which means that beside the four flavours — sweet, sour, salty, bitter — "strong" is our cuisine's unique character that makes the fifth flavour. This way Hungarian kitchen is a bit related to the Asian culture.

Lunch is the main meal and it is very typical to have at least two dishes, always starting with a warm soup, followed by the main dish which is most often meat. If a foreigner wants to look for something Hungarian here, I would say in Hungarian food culture meat has the leading role. Meat of almost any kind, even the strangest parts of animals get processed, like lungs, liver, heart or kidney, even the nose of a pig. Other basic ingredients are potato, onion, paprika and cabbage. The most well-known national dish is goulash and stew, but I think it is a shame to miss langos, white bread, potato pasta, pork cheese, ratatouille or fish soup if you happen to visit Hungary...

HOW DO YOU THINK DISHWARE AND KITCHENWARE HAVE REFASHIONED MAN'S IDEA ABOUT FOOD AND THE OTHER WAY ROUND?

While most other things are optional, eating is a basic need for everyone. We express ourselves by what we do. Since everyone eats, the expression of ourself comes from what we eat and how we do it. I feel food deserves

our respect and eating in style is a way of doing so. Nice kitchenware to honour and respect our food. A nice tea deserves a nice cup and we all deserve a nice cup of tea. It is my sensation, my choice.

YOU HAVE RECENTLY SHIFTED YOUR CREATIVE ENERGY FROM GENERAL HOUSEHOLD PRODUCTS TO DISHWARE DESIGN. WHAT IS THE DRIVE BEHIND? WHAT DO YOU WISH TO ACHIEVE THROUGH YOUR DISHES?

Actually I have always been interested in dishware design. Recently I got the opportunity to work in porcelain factories that produce dishware, on different levels from standard productions to the high quality luxury products. It was very inspiring, and I started to play with the objects I came across in the production.

I would say my focus is usually on objects that can fit into a hand. It might be the close connection, the fit-to-grab size, the technical limits. My hand is my best measurement, my channel to the material world, to touch, to feel. Object for table is a smaller group of this kind. Objects on table with function are usually about food and eating, connected to everyone, and used every day.

'TOUCH' IS A SIGNIFICANT FOCUS IN YOUR DESIGNS. WHAT DO YOU INTEND TO ADD TO THE COFFEE/TEA MOMENTS WITH THOSE SENSUAL AND PLAYFUL TOUCHES?

For me it is natural. Touch is the channel I communicate most after my eyes, so do most of us. Human's relation to heat is something I find very fascinating. It's also a basic need of mankind, the temperature we feel comfortable in.

Coffee and tea is hot. It is the main things important to highlight. Make it safe to feel the heat without burn. Let me sense by touch physically, and also mentally.

WHAT IS THE MOST DIFFICULT PART OF YOUR CREATION? WHAT ARE THE NECESSARY STEPS TO TAKE BEFORE A NEW PRODUCT COME TO LIFE?

My complexity is the most difficult to deal with in my work, my personality of contrasts. I'm always on both sides of contrasts, making functional object with an artistic drive, or the other way around.

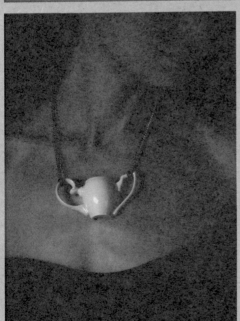

Table-wear (2010) - Pendants, rings and bangles taking on concepts and functionality of classic porcelain ware designs. Manufactured by Kahla Porzellan GmbH, Germany.

Caffe Latte (2010) - Composition of coffee pot, milk jar and sugar jar to optimise
the moments one could share with friends during their precious coffee breaks.
Manufactured by Kahla Porzellan GmbH, Germany.

Photo / Gunter Binsack

Tea for Two (2010) – Teapot integrated with an extra opening and sugar bowl, matched with customised saucers to turn tea breaks into special moments. Manufactured by Kahla Porzellan GmbH, Germany.

Coffee-Spot Espresso Cups (2010) - Porcelain espresso cups with flock-covered grooves to enhance the touch and eliminate the heat. Manufactured by Kahla Porzellan GmbH, Germany.

Hugcups (2010) - Cup with a twisted handle to increase user's physical contact with the cup. Manufactured by Kahla Porzellan GmbH, Germany.

I am complicated, and I show this complexity in simplicity. There is always so much in one piece. Take hugcups as an example. It is a game with shape and function. It is fun, unexpected, surprising, and strange. But in some ways it is bloody serious and very reasonable. It is a suitable product for someone with osteoarthritis without feeling outcast because of his special needs. It is a concept and a product, a symbol of not forgetting life is fun, sign of help and hope for the disable. It's new, but it is also so very simple as anyone could think of it although still haven't. And it is a technical achievement too.

The process usually takes time. Time might not be a procedure as such, but it is an important ingredient. Some projects start slow, coming along from my mind silently before they slowly take space, desire my attention and demand a shape. Other ideas come from who-knows-where, quickly and spontaneously. Usually when there is material in my hands. Physical work and creative thinking fuel each other. The idea is one thing. A good thing, a good start.

I like to start with a notion, an idea of what I want to achieve but it is through constant dialogue with the material from which things take shape. Ceramics require knowledge, attention and endless patience. I rely on my senses — touch, smell, sight... and respect for the material. Working with porcelain is a time-consuming occupation, and all powerful elements are involved — earth, water, air, fire, time and myself. All these are necessary to go through and consider during the process. We compromise and work together. I start a piece, and they finish it.

WHAT SEEMS TO BE THE NEW DIRECTIONS AND CRITERIA IN DESIGNING KITCHEN AND DINING TOOLS TODAY?

I think connectedness and sustainability are two important considerations in designing for the future. So much in our life is about being connected. While we are connected to the digital world 24/7 I feel it is important to keep us grounded at the present and connected to the here and now. Simple objects might trigger this. Having a nice cup of tea with a friend keeps us connected and grounded. A nice meal or a cup of tea can place us in the present, giving us much needed time for thought and meditation.

Sustainability comes as a natural topic when discussing food. Sustainable farming and use of our resources.

Food is also about sustaining ourselves. Respecting food is respecting ourselves and our world. I feel it is very important that designing for food adds to this respect.

WHAT KIND OF NEW ELEMENTS DO YOU WISH TO BRING INTO YOUR NEXT PROJECTS, AND WHY?

Objects we trust and love because the world is getting so impersonal; and playfulness, but use more and more professional solutions for the simple ideas, new technical achievements. I wish to bring the elements of the real world to people's life, as when ceramics bring in earth, air, water, fire, the past and the future all at a time.

I like challenges. I wish I could design a plate that helps my brother to eat slower; a bowl that can convince a child to like broccoli and dishware that makes an anorexic enjoy food.

I don't want to design umpteen plate with a new pattern. I want something more, not just a plate, not only an object, but a lovable object. I want you to remember this object; I want you to want it, to love it, to use it, to keep it for many years and pass on to your grandkids. I want to design a part of your day, part of your life.

IS THERE SOMETHING ABOUT FOOD OR THE FOOD CULTURE THAT YOU WOULD BE EAGERLY EXPECTING TO SEE OR TASTE?

I'm quite particular in what I like. I always try to find things I can relate to on a personal level. Things that speak to me and make me feel at home and special by using it. I usually find this in the details. The one little thing that just completes the piece. I am probably a kind of person who is looking for a little piece of home in everything. Something that feels it is made for me.

On top of that I would expect something that could...

· Keep me alive. Satisfy my sensations.
· Give me energy for new creations every day.
· Feed my eyes with beauty, my nose with sweet smell and my soul with warm joy.
· Calm my mind, convince me that I'm eating healthy.
· Give harmony to me through my body.

Special Credits / Michael Madjus

HIDDEN ANIMAL TEACUPS
imm Living

Hidden Animal Teacups are the bodily form of the designer's childhood fantasy about having wonderful guests emerging from her drink as she drank up. This collection has invited a fox, an owl and a bear to sit in the cups.

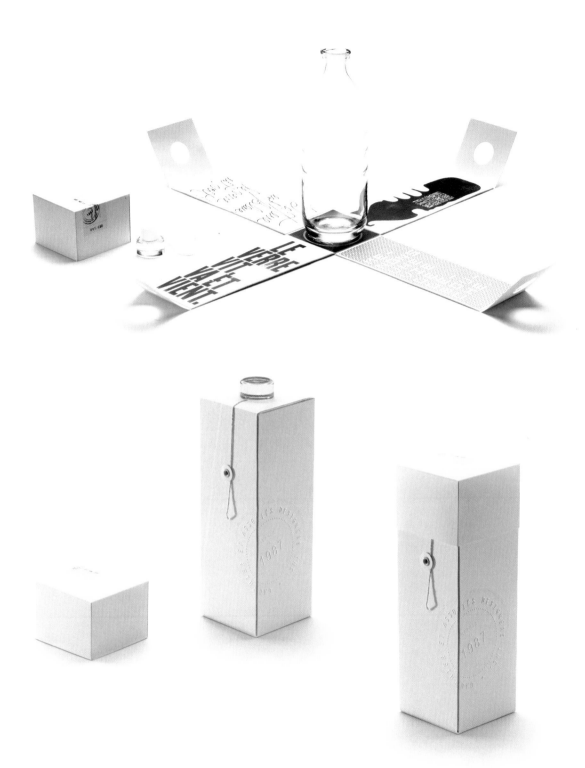

GAUTHIER BOTTLE
Gauthier Designers

Copywriting / Marie Gaudreau
Printing / Production JG

Wrapped in a white cardboard box created on the theme of resistance, Gauthier's New Year message to
clients was embraced in a thick glass bottle that is far superior to plastic containers by all means. Once
unstrung, the box blossoms to reveal a call to phrase out plastics and opt for glass.

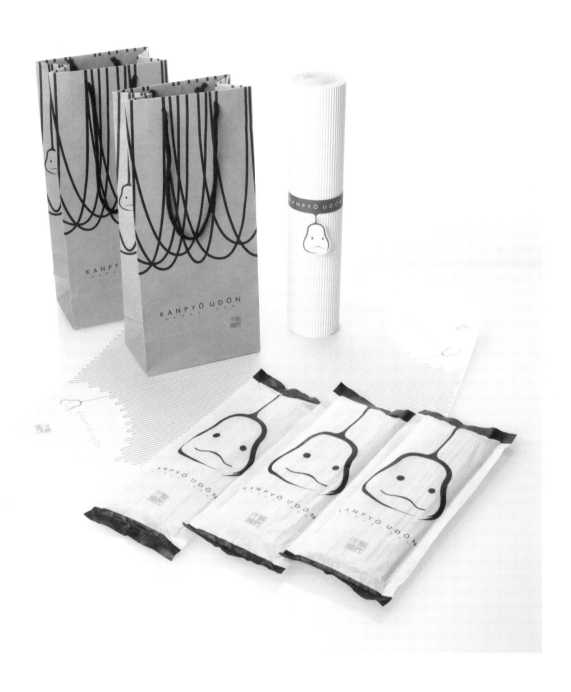

KANPYO UDON
Nosigner

Udon is the leitmotiv of the entire design. Appearing as a ceaseless piece of udon on the wrap, dangling noodles on the bag and dry udon on the corrugated gift package, the lines impart quality in every way. Also a major produce in Oyama where the udon is made, a gourd gives a friendly smile on every pack.

MULTI-NOODLES
Korefe

Like nails, screws, nuts and bolts, *Multi-Noodles* presents four short pastas in a plastic toolbox,
with different compartments to highlight the variety. Illustrative graphics visualise how the pastas
grip sauces with their unique chambers, co-developed with a small family business in Austria.

NYC SPAGHETTI
Alex Creamer

3D Modelling / Ben Thorpe

Good cooking requires good crafts and quality food is the soul of culinary art. While the pasta content is compared to the prominent Chrysler Building in New York City, visuals are kept to a minimum on the packaging to let the spaghetti itself be the clear standout.

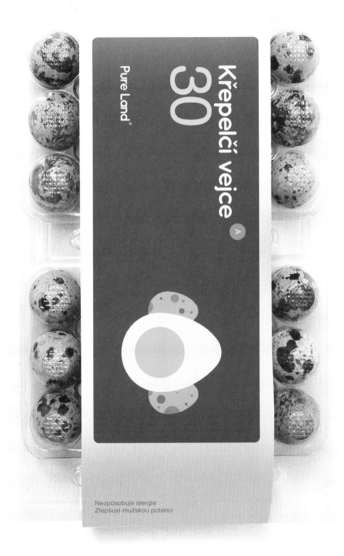

Creasence has developed a simple yet compelling wrapper for Pure Land's quail eggs. Visually clean, the wrapper sets the little eggs apart from the common perception of quail eggs as delicacy with bright graphic against a warm ash tone. The plastic carton has a capacity of 30 eggs.

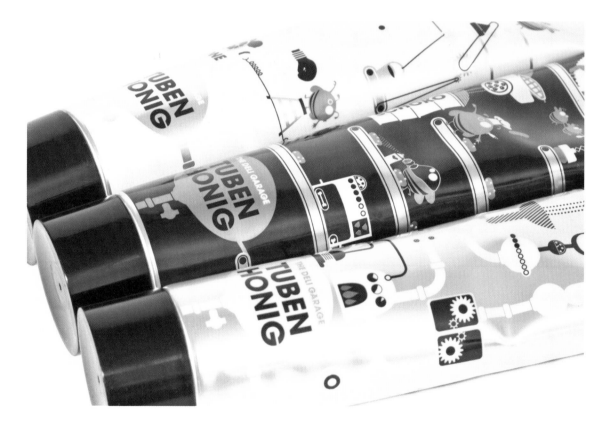

HONEY TUBES
Korefe

Shunning all sticky situations in kitchens or at barbecues, acacia honey can now be applied to fish,
meat, bread and tea directly from a tube, without recourse to honey dippers or spoons. The tiny
graphics are a tribute to the honey bees' hard work that attribute to the honey's delicate taste.

OLIVE ÖIL
Korefe

Commonly used to hold lubricants in garages, oil injection bottles find their second purpose as oil dispenser for The Deli Garage's *Olive Öil* in three flavours. The product is developed in hands with a small family-business oil producer in Catalonia, Spain.

CHOCOLATE GLUE
Korefe

Bottled in the classic wood glue bottle is 200 ml of hazelnut praline with an exquisitely high cocoa content, which can be used to write or draw on your bread or dessert, thanks to its industrial glue dispenser. *Chocolate Glue* comes in two flavours — chocolate and chocolate-biscuit.

FOOD FINISH

Korefe

Food Finish is a refreshing take on food colouring. Delivered in a paint can comparable to the industrial paint sprayers, this product offers an easy grip and control for food colouring with a range of metallic tints to glam up all manner of luxurious and culinary feasts.

BREAD
Ryohei Yoshiyuki to job

Clients / Fukuryoku Techo (Magazine).
TURNER COLOUR WORKS Co.,Ltd. (Paint Company)
Modelling / Mana Harada
Styling / Mai Narita, Yuriko Kodama
Special Credits / PANTALOON, SKKY

Many think 'painting' belongs to classrooms but *Bread* takes reference to local expressions to urge
Japanese to pick up their paint brush again like when they "paint" bread with jam and butter. The
project was created for paint producer TURNER COLOUR WORKS Co.,Ltd..

SLICED BREAD
Burak Kaynak

These notebooks might literally be the best thing since sliced bread. Numbered from one to 12, the notebooks might as well be a diary set that will make a slice of your life. Manage your thoughts and feelings systematically now, with one for each month.

ANTI-THEFT LUNCH BAGS
the.

Anti-Theft Lunch Bags are zipper bags that are good at disguising freshly prepared lunch as spoiled food with moss-like green splotches printed on both sides. They work to deceive sticky-fingered coworkers and schoolyard bullies when they desire some free lunch treats.

SLIM CHIPS
HAF

Slim Chips explore snack alternatives that aim to fill stomaches with a minimal intake of fat. The basic ingredient here is edible paper, almost nutritionless but completely fat-free. It's said to be like eating tasty air, available in mint flavour, blueberry, cheddar or wasabi.

FROM SCRATCH
Judith Klausner

Photo / Steve Pomeroy

These embroideries are Klausner's internal quest for the long-forgotten experience of making by hand from scratch, like how women had to prepare meals for their families before any packaged food come into view. Klausner's work is also about choice. She has chosen to marry these things with art.

EGGY CANDLE
KaCaMa Design Lab

The idea of producing candles out of eggshells arose as designers of KaCaMa saw the amount of eggshells discarded during food production on a regular basis. Eggshells are collected from a local bakery, Kamburs Cake Shop, washed and cleaned before soy wax and wicks are added.

KITCHEN BLOCKS
Torafu Architects

Photo / Takumi Ota
Production / IZUTSU-YA
Exhibition / AXIS GALLERY

Perhaps the worsening state of natural forest could best illustrate how we have put forest out of our mind. To bring back good memories with practicality, *Kitchen Blocks* are created for *Feeling the Forest For 12 Days* by moretrees, with 12 wooden blocks as coaster and timer, etc., in a tray.

JERRY
Sebastian Bergne Ltd

Jerry is a comical rendering of a classic setup that goes cheek by jowl with cheese in many cartoons that Bergne has watched. The cheese board is manufactured from a handsome chunk of beech by Sebastian Bergne Ltd.

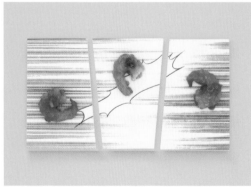

MANGA PLATES
Tsutai Mika

Cast into a sequence of shapes like manga panels, *Manga Plates* compose an exciting story when
food is arranged accordingly to the frames. Typically in black and white, each frame reveals a spate of
action details, verging on rapid zooms and stop motions with varying sound graphic effects.

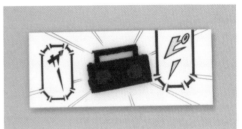

FOOD FIGHTERS
Rafael Morgan

Manufacture / fiftytwoways

Armed with grenades and machine guns, two sets of troops are destined to fight on a special battlefield and sent home safe and sound. Geared with little sticks underneath their boots, these toy soldiers are trained to secure themselves to the giant fruits when they are fresh to eat.

UTENSIL

CUTLERY TOOLKIT
Rafael Morgan

Deceptively simple, the hand tool panel is a cutlery kit that can be served as a chopping board where knives can be kept. Rooted in Morgan's fascination with the outline of hand tools in the garage, the concept is realised as a space-saver and surprise in kitchen.

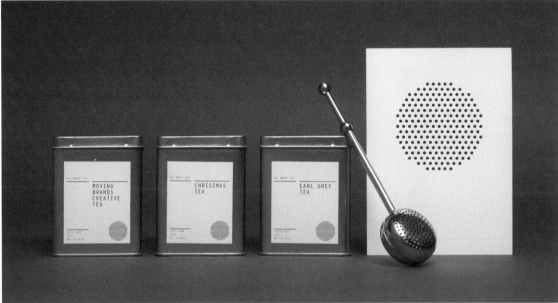

ALL ABOUT TEA
Moving Brands

Photo / Adam Laycock

Blending and straining are the essential steps to brew a good tea. Taking the perforated pattern of strainers for fine brews, the bold yet simplistic symbol spotlights the founder's passion and intricacies of tea as a stamp of quality in its existing wholesale market and new retail channels.

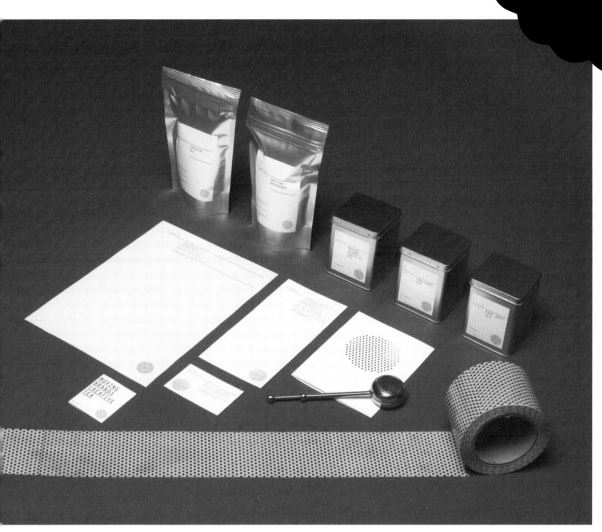

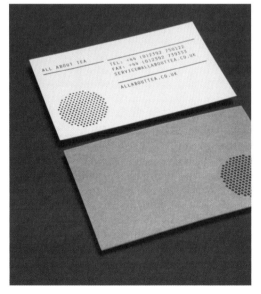

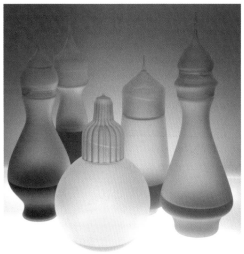

MINARETS
Hamilton Turksoy

Named 'Minarets', which originally describes the distinctive conical crown structure of Islamic mosques, the handmade glass decanters are inspired by scrap glass pieces found at a glassblowing workshop in London. The domed caps can double as a glass to hold drinks.

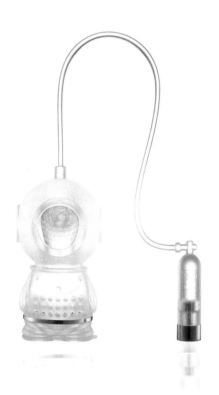

TEA DIVER
AbelPartners Design Studio

Tea diver has its inspiration drawn from Leonardo da Vinci's diving apparatus design where tea leaves in lieu of air can be trapped inside. The flavour of the flowers or tea are to be infused into the water through the little pores on its face-mask.

TEA FISHING
AbelPartners Design Studio

Tea Fishing offers tea lovers a fuss-free chance to bide their time while they make their tea. Coming in a pair, the kids are designed to sit tight at the edge of the cup and hook the tea bag's string to the fishing pod until the tea is ready to drink.

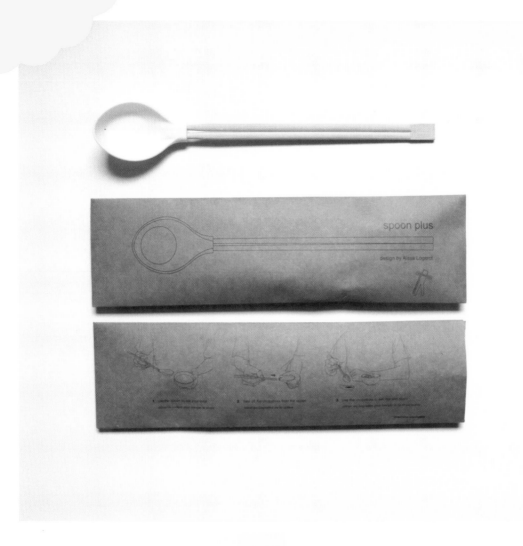

SPOONPLUS
Aïssa Logerot

When a spoon meets chopsticks, it becomes *Spoonplus*, primarily fashioned for the degustation of Asian meals, or Japanese meals in particular, where multiple courses would be introduced with a soup. If used separately, the tiny shallow bowl can work as a saucer and chopstick rest.

DIN-INK
ZO_loft architecture & design

Din-ink is a hybrid of pen cap and knife, fork or spoon that can be carried around easily for a green lunch break. Made from completely recyclable and sustainable materials, the cutlery set is designed to fit a range of popular ballpoint pens most common in offices.

DALIAN
Peter Ibruegger

Photo / Toby Summerskill

A stylish moustache or a decent bow tie are often reliable indicators of a man's fashionable
instinct. Carrying two designs on one mug, *DALIAN* offers multiple ways to complete party-goers'
look with a bowler hat sugar bowl that doubles as a lid to keep the tea warm.

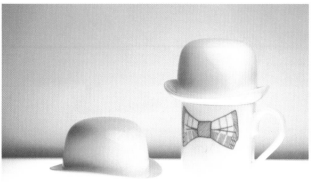

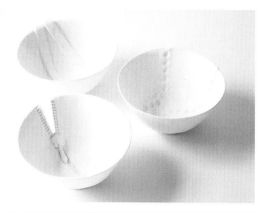

DRESSED FOR DINNER
studioooij

In a lighthearted way, this dinnerware set illustrates an extension of the social aspects of dining
into a dinner's wardrobe. Be it a romantic date or a formal business dinner, anticipation, attraction
and seduction are all as much part of the relish as the food itself.

TINY LANDSCAPE
Yukihiro Kaneuchi

A new product is always like a new journal — blank and pure — waiting to be personalised with memories and thoughts. Like coffee stains but enriched with a beautiful story, the patchy mark predicts a user-cup relationship in a narrative scene.

TABLE DISH COVER
MAEZM

Integrated with dishware of different size and purpose, *Table Dish Cover* is a pliable, injection-moulded silicon sheet that can be spread out anywhere to start a meal and washed after use. This item measures 505 mm by 415 mm by 57 mm.

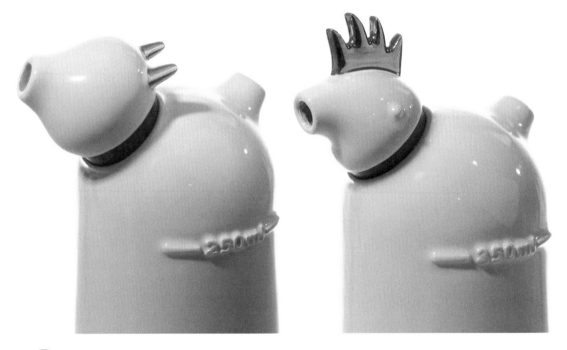

PIDOG AND DUCKSTER
StudioKahn

Paired with pointed ears or a comb, these ceramic oil and vinegar vessel sets feature a silicon
seal like a soggy pig's snout. Whether it is a pig or a dog, a duck or a rooster depends on how
you look at its head.

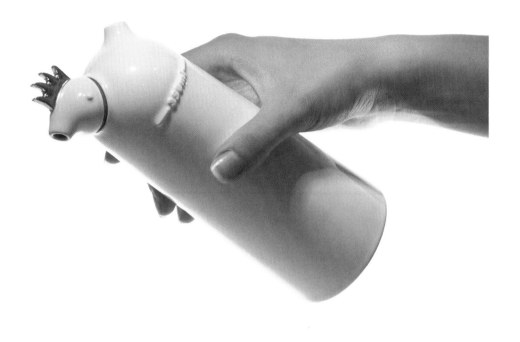

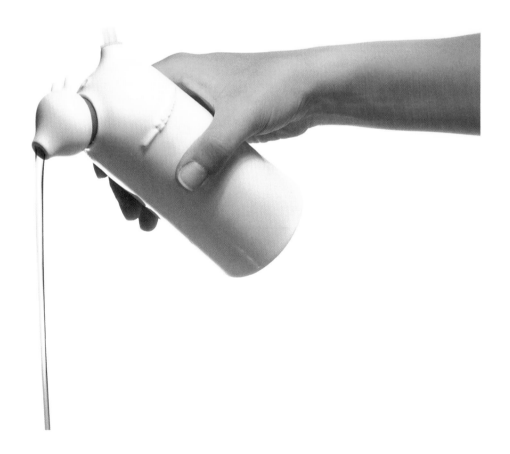

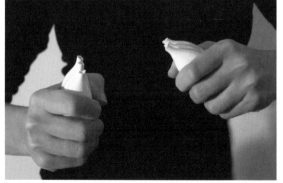

FRAGILE
StudioKahn

Photo / Oded Antman

Breaking might often be a result of an impulsive outburst, but this time it is more like a constructive one than destroys. Coming in one piece, this ceramic salt and pepper set urges end-users to complete the design by snapping it into halves.

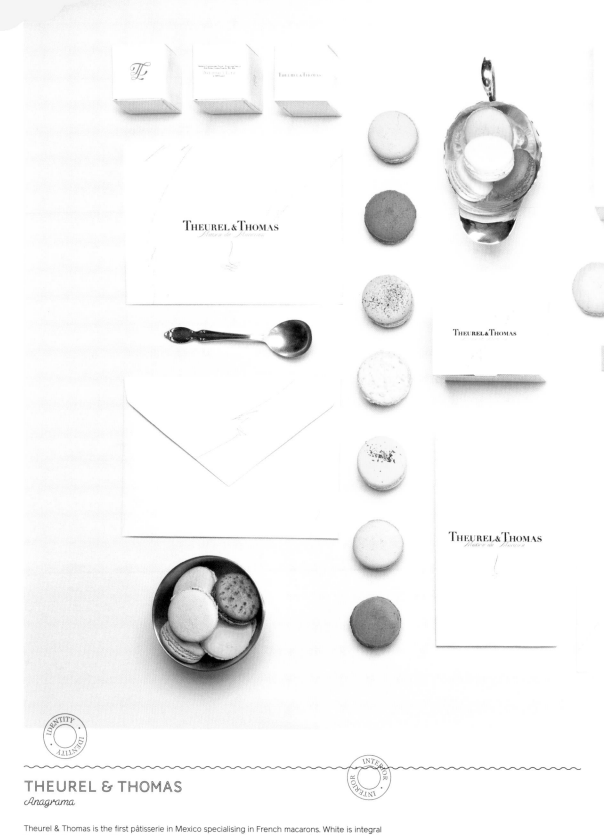

THEUREL & THOMAS
Anagrama

Theurel & Thomas is the first pâtisserie in Mexico specialising in French macarons. White is integral to both its branding and interior directions to set off the vibrancy and elegance of this delicate dessert. A hint of French is imparted in its Didot types and its cyan and magenta decor.

THEUREL & THOMAS

THEUREL & THOMAS

THEUREL & THOMAS

THEUREL & THOMAS

MCFANCY
Access Agency

McFancy is an upmarket version of McDonald's store specially launched to coincide with fashion weeks. Part art installation and part gathering spot, the temporary eatry gives event attendants a stylish nod with a traditional McDonald's menu served in playful yet elegant packaging designs.

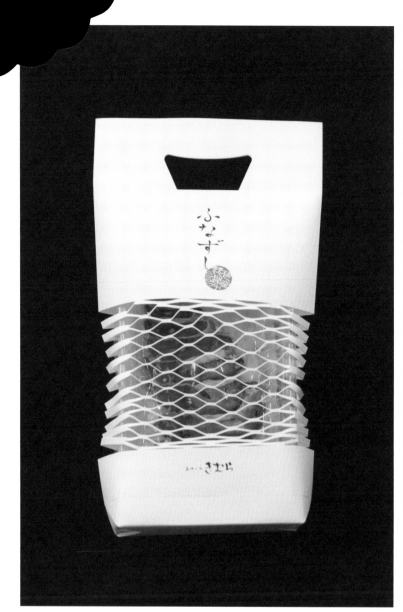

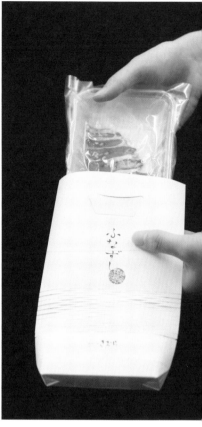

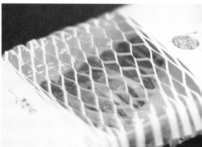

FUNAZUSHI
Masahiro Minami Laboratory

Design / Shuji Hikawa
Photo / Masahiro Minami

Delicate like a paper sculpture with a fish scale pattern revealed as the fish slides in, the package reveals a "Funazushi", a traditional fermented fish in vacuum packaging originating from Shiga Prefecture, Japan. The fin-shaped handle offers a subtle hint at the product inside.

SLOWLY DOES IT
BERG

Sourcing produce from local boutique farmers, SLOWLY DOES IT's packaging design is consistent with their environmentally-responsible approach to quality food. The owner's promise is made solid with the his own quote printed on the store's craft paper bags in a robust typeface.

BASANTI
Menosunocerouno

Mexican gourmet tea brand, BASANTI, believes rediscovering wellness in premium drinks is modern luxury. Creating a strong tension between the relaxed handwritten logo and polished surfaces, the packaging is designed to bring a unique brand experience with style.

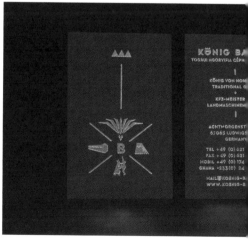

AKOSOMBO BEER
Deutsche & Japaner Creative Studio

Photo / Mirka Laura Severa

King Bansah is a Ludwigshafen-based African king and Akosombo Beer is one of his efforts to fund his aid projects back in Ghana. Its label is an extension of the king's corporate identity which underlines his authenticity and lordliness in a range of gold-foiled icons over black.

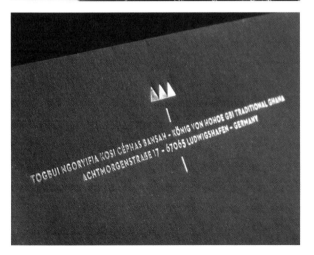

CAPITAL KITCHEN
Cornwell

Capital Kitchen is a homewares and food retailer opened to complement the luxury wing of Chadstone Shopping Centre. Stylised as a modern farmhouse in a mix of nostalgic food items, the store looks to transport its shoppers to a time in history when everything went slower and less chaotic.

THE HAND BURGER
Couple

Entirely produced out of paper, The Hand Burger identity highlights the artistry of making a good burger completely by hand. The versatile double-decker takeaway packaging is specially designed to keep the tomato slice chilled and buns spongy even when they are not relished right away.

FREE MIDI STRAWBERRY
MILKSHAKE WITH EVERY
PURCHASE OF THE
HARDBURGER ORIGINAL

RAFFLES CITY SHOPPING CENTRE, B1-77/78

FOR DINE-IN ONLY. OFFER VALID TILL 13TH SEPTEMBER 2009.
NOT VALID WITH OTHER PROMOTIONAL OFFERS. WHILE STOCKS LAST.
WE RESERVE THE RIGHT TO AMEND THE TERMS OF THE PROMOTION AT ANY TIME WITHOUT PRIOR NOTICE.

THE
HARD
BURGER

MENU

THE HARDBURGER ORIGINAL	$13.8
TEA SMOKED DUCK BURGER	$15.8
CHICKEN CAESAR BURGER	$12.8
TANDOOR CHICKEN BURGER	$13.8
PULLED PORK BURGER	$11.8
PARMESAN PRAWNCAKE BURGER	$17.8
BEER BATTERED DORY BURGER	$14.8
STUFFED PORTOBELLO BURGER	$13.8
VEGETARIAN KAKIAGE BURGER	$10.8
THE WORKS BURGER	$16.8
EVERYTHING ELSE	
DRINKS AND DESSERTS	

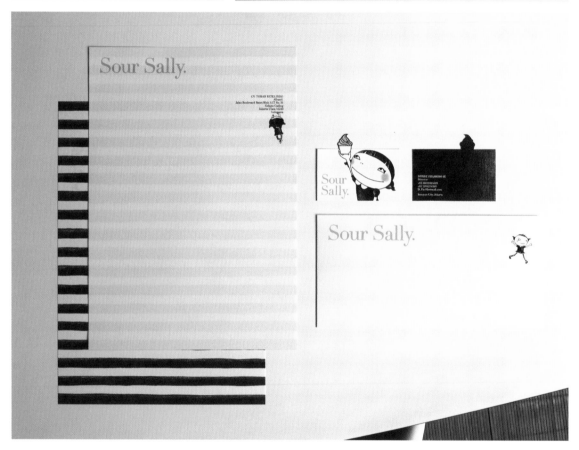

SOUR SALLY
Kinetic Singapore

Photo / VisualMind

Frozen yogurt appeals with its chill and low-fat content. To convey a delightful surrounding for the sweet treat for all, Sally was introduced to kindle some fun in her store and patrons with her bright character and favourite zebra stripes across the store's interior and stationery suite.

Sour Sally.

WHOOPEE! IT'S YOGURT TIME!

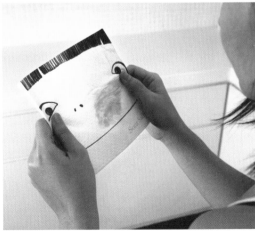

THE REEL CATCH
Jesse Harris

Sustainability is central to The Reel Catch's identity design. While the wrapper is intended for single use, its goal is to minimise waste and ensure the food does not rot quicker at the same time. Its philosophy is upheld by original gyotaku-style illustrations of their daily catches.

MEAT&
BREAD

MEAT & BREAD
Glasfurd & Walker

Interior / Craig Stanghetta

IDENTITY

Gastown's latest addition to Vancouver is a sandwich shop with focus on its day-to-day roasts.
To highlight the meat, four animal icons and a daily special sticker were created for the sandwich
wrap. Strength through simplicity was the ultimate mandate in this identity system design.

FEMA   FEMA

U.S. FEDERAL EMERGENCY MANAGEMENT AGENCY
Ludvig Bruneau Rossow

Photo / John Tøsse Kolvik

FEMA is a fictitious agency that would remain in function for survivors in 2030 after the world is completely destroyed. With focus on direct communication, FEMA has its logo applied on vintage green for documents and supplies to establish a clear link with a coordinated look

LETTHEMSITCAKE!
Kabiljo Inc.

Photo / Francesco Troina,
Christian Maricic

Drawing on the finest Viennese food traditions passed down from princess Marie Antoinette's era,
the sofa stands for abundance, growth and sweetness – the Austrian sustainability amidst economic
woes. The two-seaters are built from fake wheat bags topped with chocolate icing made of sponge.

1

ZERO
Hasegawa Yoshio

Fashioned into a mound of bent soda cans, Hasegawa's paper sculptures challenge the compe-
tence of paper in intricate details and forms. Featuring netted details, each structure is handcrafted
out of paper and acrylic, giving the cans a surprisingly natural cast.

1 / Catch the Zero
(Photo / Maya Tatsukawa)
2 / Sloughs
3 / The Birth of Vacuity
(Photo / Keiko Gallery)
4 / One of Zero

2

3

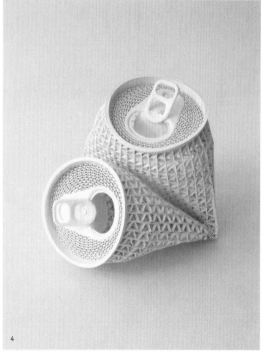

4

WHAT CAME FIRST?
Kyle Bean

Inspired by cycles and sustainability, *What Came First?* is Bean's tongue-in-cheek interpretation of
the eternal question, built using the most appropriate material — egg shells. The sculpture remains
fragile and stands over 20 centimetres in height.

FROM SPONTANEITY TO MINIATURE SETUP

Christopher Boffoli uses his journalistic instinct to satirise in visual art

HOW WOULD YOU REGARD FOOD AND ITS RELATIONSHIP TO MANKIND?

First, people obviously need food to provide sustenance. There is something very human when we sit down to a plate of food. And, the continued popularity of cooking over open fires (despite the option not to cook that way) tells me that there is also something still very primal about cooking and eating. It has no doubt been man's success at finding and producing food that has put us at the top of the food chain. It often astounds me how much diversity of foodstuffs there is in the world. It is incredible how many things are available for us to eat, and how those things can be almost infinitely combined to make different foods and flavours. It really is remarkable. Food is one of the most accessible parts of most cultures. Even when people might disagree politically or philosophically, or speak different languages, food is something that comes across more readily and translates with much more ease. For many people, experiencing the foods of other cultures is a "gateway drug" of sorts into that culture.

Conversely, though man is no doubt the number one predator in the world, food in the modern world has become a much more complicated thing than a simple source of sustenance. Somehow in the last century in the United States, food has transformed into something that we not only need to keep us alive but that potentially can kill us. Food science and the industrialisation of

foods has made the production of foodstuffs easier and more efficient. But it sometimes comes at a significant environmental and biological cost. For instance, genetically modified foods endeavour to use science to reduce or eliminate the use of pesticides, which may either be harmless or have long-term genetic effects that we will only understand in time. Certain vegetables have been bred for appearance and heartiness, making seasonal foods available year round. Though variety and flavour often suffer. And corporations have learned to produce crops like potatoes and bananas in a way that ensures year-round consistency and quality. But the "monocultures" used to produce those crops have pushed out the benefits of natural selection and genetic diversity, making those crops especially vulnerable to natural challenges like fungi.

The United States consumes a percentage of the world's resources that is out of proportion with the size of its population. And this surplus of resources allows the US to produce a great surplus of calories for its citizens to a level that causes widespread problems, including obesity and other catastrophic health issues. Crops like corn have been so successful that the government routinely manipulates the production of the crop to control pricing and surpluses at a time when many in the rest of the world scramble for a minimum amount of calories each day. Corn in particular, with its ties to use for ethanol fuel and sweeteners like high-fructose corn syrup, has

become an extremely complicated food source and part of some very complicated and politicised systems.

So, at least in North America, our relationship to food is at once essential and dysfunctional.

HOW DOES THIS RELATIONSHIP INFLUENCE YOUR CREATION?

On its face, my work is something that is whimsical and humorous. But of course there are deeper messages there too. Like many Americans, the tiny figures in my work are surrounded by an abundance of food, which presents issues that I think are worth exploring: over-consumption, waste, excessive portion sizes, reliance of food as a psychological crutch, etc. I'm always interested to hear how people react when they see my images from this series. I often hear people say things like "I wish I lived in a world with giant pieces of chocolate cake". But the reality is that too much of a good thing is actually a burden. Even our favourite foods would sicken us if we had to eat large quantities of it, or ate it and nothing else. So in a sense the work is a response to surplus and the truth about getting exactly what we want. Our desire in the face of abundance is often out of sync with reality.

HOW WOULD YOU DESCRIBE THE FOOD CULTURE IN THE STATES? WHAT SHOULD A FOREIGNER LOOK FOR IF THEY VISIT YOUR COUNTRY ONE DAY?

I think probably every ethnic group that came to America brought something that in some ways changed and influenced the culture of food and flavors of America. We often describe our culture as a "melting pot" where everyone blends into one culture. But it would be more accurate to compare ourselves to a tossed salad, in which all of the components blend together while still retaining their own colour and flavour.

The culture of food is fluid. Newer generations continue to hold on to (and evolve) recipes that were handed down to us. Of course, the selection and preparation of food in my modern kitchen is drastically different than that of my great-grandparents. I have access to an en-tirely more diverse selection of foods than my ancestors would have had only a few decades ago. And my access to food knowledge and learning is also much more global and broad. But food is still the strongest cultural tie I have to my antecedents. I might not even have detailed

stories about the life of my great-grandparents. But I do have the recipes they left behind.

What's interesting and somewhat sad is that, despite the fact that Americans have access to hundreds if not thousands of foodstuffs, there has paradoxically been a devolution of knowledge and interest in cooking. My great-grandmother spent much of her life in the kitchen, cooking and baking from scratch, because she had no other choice. Modern convenience and the pace of modern life mean that I spend less time in the kitchen. I have many more choices. And yet my great-grandmother had skills and food intuition that I am lacking due to those convenience.

Food is a constant in our culture. Our need for food, and our interest in food as a subject is undiminished. But our relationship to food, and its place in our life is very different. In modern America, food is no longer confined to set meal times in the dining room. Americans eat in classrooms, at their desks at work, in their cars. Food is all around us. But food is increasingly something we eat but do not prepare (and certainly do not grow) ourselves. In the United States we have entire television networks filled with shows about food and cooking. Every year publishers release hundreds of new cookbooks. But somehow, all of that attention is more channelled towards being food spectators and consumers, as opposed to food producers and cooks. It is a very odd reality.

Also paradoxical is that, despite people having more information and access than ever to foods and cuisines from around the world, many Americans eat a weekly diet of bland, processed foods that don't change very much from week to week. Though there has surely been an advance in the prevalence of farmers markets, green markets and organic food stores, they tend to be frequented more by better educated people who live in urban environments with more disposable income. The broad majority of middle-class Americans are probably the demographic that most relies on pre-packaged, pro-cessed foods. I honestly cannot understand why there is such a reliance on sameness and habit at a time when we are, more than ever, food spectators. But that is my assessment of the current state of American food culture and something that certainly motivated my work.

Disparity · Big Appetites (2007-2011) - Personal project inspired by modern American food culture and accomplished in Seattle, Washgington.

WHAT IS THE MOST BEAUTIFUL THING ABOUT FOOD? HOW DOES IT INSPIRE YOU AND YOUR WORK?

The choice of food as a backdrop was absolutely a conscious choice as food (paired with toys) is very accessible, regardless of culture, language or social status. Food can be very beautiful — with wonderful textures and colours — which works very well for macro photography. And as it is a part of nature, where colours always coordinate with each other and never clash, food can be a very satisfying and pleasing in terms of colour space. But beyond that, food, like toys, is one of the most common things to just about everyone in the world. Everyone on earth has played with toys and eaten food from the very earliest age. So combining these two elements in a way that plays with scale has obviously been a very powerful platform for telling a story and presenting an idea.

DISPARITY IS QUITE A DIFFERENT ATTEMPT COMPARED TO YOUR OTHER PORTFOLIOS. HOW DID YOU COME UP WITH THE IDEA?

I have always been interested in size disparity and a juxtaposition of scales between people and the environment around them. It seemed to be a very popular device in television and movies that I saw as a kid in the late 70's and early 80's (like Sid and Marty Krofft's show *Dr. Shrinker*, and films like *The Incredible Shrinking Woman*, *Honey I Shrunk the Kids*, *Innerspace*, etc). Long before that, from the earliest days of cinema, filmmakers were exploiting the dramatic effects of having tiny characters fleeing from, say, horrifyingly giant insects. Of course, the concept goes back hundreds of years earlier, with the Lilliputians in Jonathan Swift's *Gulliver's Travels* in the 18th century. It seems at once a timeless and versatile theme, whether employed for a summer popcorn movie or social satire circa 1726. There is something about this concept of size disparity that people find compelling.

Childhood is a time spent actually living in an out-of-scale adult world. And a child's world is further populated with even smaller toys. Like many young boys, I built meticulously detailed scale models. I also had a large collection of Matchbox cars. When I was about eight, my father built a large model railroad in our basement. Everything about the train layout was incredibly detailed. It featured a complete town with electric lights and flashing railroad crossings. There was an almost god-like feeling

of standing at the controls, orchestrating the animated pageant of this tiny world, rearranging everything at any capricious whim. My parents had a tumultuous marriage and my siblings and I often felt like we were living in a war zone. But everything was always quiet, clean and perfect in the tiny world of the basement trains.

So I had thought about the mix of scales for a long time, and was familiar with the figures for decades. But it all came together when I saw some large dioramas, by the Chapman Brothers, at the Saatchi Gallery in London back in 2002. It used hundreds of handmade figures in rather disturbing and horrific battle scenes. It was somewhat hard to approach (which I think is a good thing and something art can and should do to challenge us) but wonderfully executed. An even stronger influence was a work called *Travelers* by Walter Martin & Paloma Muñoz, who used tiny figures in fantastical (and sometimes dark and troubling) scenes inside snow globes.

THERE ARE FRUSTRATIONS, ROMANCE AND DISCOVERIES IN BETWEEN THE STORYLINES. WHAT ARE YOU TRYING TO PICTURE IN THIS COLLECTION?

The breadth of the image series has really unfolded rather organically. Despite what I've said before, there has not been a lot of strategy in terms of a top loaded, didactic message. One of my favourite quotes in the book *Out of Africa* is where Karen Von Blixen wrote something like "The world was made round on purpose so that we can never see too far ahead over the horizon". I respect and appreciate that sentiment and, for the most part, aspire to live life in a way in which discoveries and surprises (and sometimes happy accidents) reveal themselves to you. While there is definitely an overarching message that informs the project as a whole, it can be just as effective to see how the images come together when fuelled by the unconscious.

Humour is one of the strongest elements, which is a natural fit as laughter is something important in my life. Sometimes the images are fed by the context afforded by the relationship between the figures and the food. I have to think about what the character is doing in the environment that makes the image work. This is often self-evident in the image (like a man mowing a large head of broccoli). In others, there is a clever caption that lends context and reinforces the humour. Like the image of the rotund man who is facing a regiment of riot police

behind French fry barricades with a cheeseburger behind them. The image works on its own to some extent. A large man who wants what he can see and is preparing to run the roadblocks of the avenue of opportunity that is presented. But then the quote is "It was the exact moment when Larry knew that those advanced Judo lessons were really going to pay off". So the quote challenges the viewer's assumption of the capabilities of the character and suggests what is going to happen next.

Some of the images are somewhat more political. I was raised Catholic and spent many years in private, parochial school. But now I'm an atheist. So some of the images reference some of my thoughts on the politics of religion, my response to what was imposed on me as a child, and where life has led me as I've grown into my own person.

THIS PROJECT IS QUITE A LONG JOURNEY CONSIDERING ITS TIME SPAN. WHAT HAS HAPPENED BETWEEN THE YEARS? DID YOU MAKE ANY INTERESTING DISCOVERIES?

The project has gotten easier and harder over time. In one way, the images have been easier to do well as I have become better at working with and lighting the food. And though the same 100mm 2.8f macro lens was used for the entire series, the camera bodies have continued to evolve over the years that I've done this work. On the other hand, it has become increasingly harder to find foods to shoot that I've not worked with yet. And though my collection of tiny figures has grown considerably, it is more of a challenge to find new figures with a fresh context. The widespread notoriety of these images was the biggest surprise as I worked on the series for many years before anyone ever cared. But at this point I realise that there are probably more images behind me than new images to be shot. Actually, I have given thought to the progression of the work and where I could take it, whether that is into scenes that are more like dioramas with multiple figures in larger scenes. I've had some requests for commercial commissions as well. However, there are many other parts of my overall creative efforts (both with editorial photography, writing and filmmaking) that I would like to which I'd like to devote attention.

HOW DO YOU FIND THE RESULTS? HOW WOULD YOU WISH TO SEE THE AUDIENCE RESPOND TO YOUR CREATION?

I'm pleased with the overall reaction to this image series, as much as the widespread notice continues to surprise me. Most often people are responding with surprise followed by humour. I wish that people would take time to understand the work beyond that, but most people don't. The nature of the Internet is that people process a high volume of information quickly and move on to something else. In some cases, people have taken the time to contact me, to ask permission to use my images on their websites or in magazines, etc. They have made the effort to understand the work as a whole. But in many more instances, people have been entertained by the images and choose to just take them, to illegally download them without permission and repost them to their own websites. In one sense they are sharing my work with a broader audience when they do this. But mostly it serves them by creating free content for their websites and generating ad revenue. So on one hand it can be validating when someone so readily accepts your work that they want to possess or share it.

Alternately, it can be violating to take the time to painstakingly create something one day, to put it online on your own artist website, only then to see it on a website the very next day being used by someone else on the other side of the world who did not show the courtesy to ask for permission first. Especially in a world filled with so much unpleasantness and difficulty, there is something of value in entertaining people and making them laugh. But I would much rather prefer to make people think about something and maybe feel something. That is a more elusive goal.

WHAT ARE YOU PLANNING TO CREATE NEXT?

The *Disparity* series is but a very small part of a large creative effort which includes other types of photography, writing, filmmaking, design, and many other creative outlets. I will perhaps continue to create images in this series if I can continue to find inspiration. There is still growing interest in this work and a demand for physical prints, notecards and other items. I have thought about where this project could possibly, logically go in terms of next steps. I have had some offers to do commercial commissions. And I did a special, limited edition print for

my best friend's film project (in an effort to raise money to make her film) which was more in the realm of a scene or diorama, going well beyond the concept of one or two figures on a single piece of food. Whether I'll continue down that road, I'm not sure. Perhaps there are more completed images behind me than ones that lie ahead. However, I know for certain that I will continue to create something. I'll always be looking, thinking, shooting pictures. It is something that comes naturally and cannot be suppressed.

IS THERE SOMETHING ABOUT FOOD OR THE FOOD CULTURE THAT YOU WOULD BE EAGERLY EXPECTING TO SEE OR TASTE?

I have been lucky to travel the world extensively. As such, I have had many exotic food experiences. So while I'm sure there are always new foods to taste, I can't say that there is anything obvious that stands out in terms of my looking forward to it or wanting to try it. Especially in the United States, where so much about our culture has to do with everything conforming to our expectations and with virtually every need or desire met with a sense of instant gratification, it is nice that we have certain foods that are still best only at certain times. Always getting what you want isn't always healthy. It is good when the scarcity of something makes it sweeter when we have to wait for it. In a world in which you are overwhelmed with choices it is only those things that exceed our expectations that have any real value.

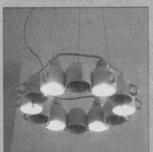

FROM PRAGMATISM TO IDEALISM

Sander Lucas demonstrates the beauty of basics in functional art

HOW WOULD YOU REGARD FOOD AND ITS RELATIONSHIP TO MANKIND?

Food is very important. In Dutch it is often referred as the "(red) thread of daily life". It's how the day flows and how we mark our entire day — from meal to meal. Without food, life would be very boring. Food is always a moment of relaxation. You will get new energy to go on with your life again.

HOW CAN INNOVATIVE PRODUCTS AND INDUSTRIAL DESIGN HELP TO DRAW THIS RELATIONSHIP CLOSER?

Products can help to experience food differently — to give food a visual context and setting. It make your meal already delicious without tasting.

It's always nice that people first see a nice glass or light and then within ten seconds they recognise the shapes and are really surprised.

WHAT IS FOOD CULTURE LIKE IN THE NETHERLANDS? WHAT SHOULD A FOREIGNER LOOK FOR IF THEY VISIT YOUR COUNTRY ONE DAY?

There are some very traditional meals like "boerenkool (vegetable with potato)" and "stamppot (carrot with potato)". Eating "haring (raw fish)" is also very Dutch and, of course, "drop (liquorice)".

Next to that people eat a lot of meat and a lot of food from different cultures.

I think there is not really a tradition or ritual – as you can see from Van Gogh's *The Potato Eaters*. In the past Dutch people eat a lot of potatoes and they still do.

During the weekends people really want to do something special, so they go out for dinner or cook a very special meal for friends. During the week people cook quickly or skip dinners from time to time.

HOW DO YOU THINK INDUSTRIAL DESIGN HAVE REFASHIONED MAN'S IDEA ABOUT FOOD AND YOUR IDEAS THE OTHER WAY ROUND?

People can really appreciate the value of industrial design — eating food already starts with the ambiance and the presentation of food is very important to get to the ultimate experience of food enjoyment.

While today's kitchen tool and storage device designs are about beauty and pleasure, it's still very important for designs to be something beautiful yet functional. Utensils and tableware are very important [in modern kitchens and on dining tables, like] a ritual what never will disappear, or maybe it will if you will just use it once a week.

When people are really enthusiastic about eating with well-designed tools and you will get a lot of positive feedback. This gives me energy to produce more wonderful products.

YOUR COLLECTION PRACTICALLY DEMONSTRATES HOW ORDINARY THINGS CAN BE PUT IN A DIFFERENT WAY. HOW DID YOU START YOUR CREATION? WHY DID YOU CHOOSE TO CREATE WITH CUTLERY AND DISHWARE?

Cutlery and dishware is the basic ingredients to eat food in our culture, everyone recognize these products/ shapes. I'm always searching for new shapes and just by trial and error there while exist new shapes. My study of "Man and Leisure" at the design academy really helped me to understand how important it is to have your own identity as a designer and what you will design must be perfect in every detail and find the essence of your creation — "less is more".

HOW DO YOU NORMALLY START WITH A NEW DESIGN? HOW DO YOU ACQUIRE THE MATERIALS YOU NEED?

This is very hard to tell. But I normally just build a lot of different things slowly [at the same time] and interesting things will come up for me to further develop into maybe a final product. This is hard to say how long it would normally take to finish a design. It could be two months or two years. Sometimes it's still not totally what you want and it takes time to improve it.

Most materials are collected from the street or a "kringloopwinkel (recycling shop)", which is also where my ideas are found.

WHAT IS THE MOST DIFFICULT PART OF YOUR CREATION? WHAT ARE THE NECESSARY STEPS TO TAKE BEFORE A NEW PRODUCT COME TO LIFE?

The most difficult part is to create something what is exactly the same feeling I have in my head, without knowing how it will look like. it's just a feeling you want to turn into a 3D product.

WHAT SEEMS TO BE THE NEW DIRECTIONS AND CRITERIA IN DESIGNING KITCHEN AND DINING TOOLS TODAY?

Craftsmanship is very important. It needs to have a personality to make it a unique piece. It must emanate a quality like you're just the only one who's got the piece.

WHAT KIND OF NEW ELEMENTS DO YOU WISH TO BRING INTO YOUR NEXT PROJECTS AND WHY?

[I've already incorporate these elements] in the most simple tiles, size 15x15cm you normally use on your (kitchen) wall. I will present it in the Dutch Design Week, which starts from 22th of October, 2011.

IS THERE SOMETHING ABOUT FOOD OR THE FOOD CULTURE THAT YOU WOULD BE EAGERLY EXPECTING TO SEE OR TASTE?

Mood food. There should be a device that could just measure your mood and they will pick/prepare the ultimate meal for that moment. I really would like [to have one of this because] if you are a little bit sad it's always hard to think about something nice to eat.

Sander Lucas Ontwerpen Collection (2006-2010) - Fixtures and house-
hold products demonstrating new functionality and aesthetics built on the
most basic and simple dishware designs.

FROM INDIVIDUALITY TO CONVIVIAL AMBIENCE

Jonas Wagell exemplifies simplicity in its most vivid form

HOW WOULD YOU REGARD FOOD AND ITS RELATIONSHIP TO MANKIND, AND THE ROLE OF DESIGN IN BETWEEN?

There has obviously been a lot of discussions about food on a moral and political level lately. The food industry has an impact on both people's health and the global environment. I will not partake in this complex debate, but believe architecture and design can serve a purpose to maintain and enhance an interest for natural and healthy food and the development of new food sources with less environmental impact. Consumerism has pushed food prices down, resulting in lower quality, unhealthy conditions and morally questionable production methods, especially in the meat industry.

Furthermore, food trends like low-carbohydrate diets increased demand for meat which requires multiple amounts of grain and vegetables as forage to produce.

WHAT IS FOOD CULTURE IN SWEDEN LIKE? WHAT SHOULD A FOREIGNER LOOK FOR IF THEY VISIT YOUR COUNTRY ONE DAY?

Sweden is a liberal country that has always been quite influenced by other cultures. In the major cities like Stockholm and Gothenburg you can find pretty much any cuisine today. However, there is a strong food heritage based on fishing and hunting, and also grain, beets

and potatoes have an important role. Some Swedish specialties originate from old preservation methods like the pickled herring, which is a must at Midsummer's festivities, or the smelly fermented herring, a specialty from northern Sweden that is salted, "soured" and canned. And of course, the Swedish meatballs always have a place on the "Smörgåsbord", the Swedish buffet.

JWDA DISPLAYS A PRIMARY FOCUS ON DESIGN FOR LIVING, SPANNING CUTLERY AND ARCHITECTURE. WHAT ARE THE BASIC PRINCIPLES THAT UNDERLIE YOUR IDEAS?

My design is focused on functional items rather than artistic objects. I appreciate products that can be used everyday and be part of people's life. I believe attraction and emotion is more important than exclusivity and quality. I try to create simplistic objects that are easy to understand and use but with something warm and human added to the form. A certain character or personal DNA, if you will. I like to call myself a generous minimalist.

THE DESIGN BAR IS VERY DIFFERENT FROM WHAT YOU DO. WHAT POPPED INTO YOUR HEAD WHEN YOU WERE FIRST APPROACHED FOR THE JOB?

I'm actually quite comfortable with these type of projects.

The Design Bar (2010) - Furnishing for a temporary café and VIP lounge at the Stockholm Furniture Fair 2010, with Jonas Wagell's own product and furniture designs.

VIP LOUNGE
the forest

DESIGN BAR
the industry

THE FOREST & THE INDUSTRY
A concept by architect and designer Jonas Wagell

DESIGN BAR
the industry

I have been working with exhibitions and corporate branding as a strategic project manager for almost a decade before going back to art school. I'm used to trade fair project that are very content and communication intense. From that perspective the Design Bar was a light-weight!

I think that's one of the reasons I aimed for a different approach than what's normally expected at a trade fair. I wanted the experience to differ from rest and feel theatrical and graphic. The high ceiling and great head-room made it a lot easier to make an impact.

THE BAR EXPLORED THE RELATIONSHIP BETWEEN "FOREST AND INDUSTRY". HOW WAS IT APPROPRIATE TO THE STOCKHOLM FURNITURE FAIR?

The project required two different areas within the same space, a VIP lounge and a public café. I wanted the two to be distinctly different and easy to tell apart, but still follow the same esthetical theme.

The relationship between forest and the industry is a metaphor for the furniture industry where raw materials are refined and transformed into objects of function and desire. Furthermore, in a society with increasing consumerism the theme aimed to pay tribute to craftsmanship and manufacturing skills in contrast to high-volume manufacture and throw-awayism.

YOU HAVE CREATED A THEATRICAL ENVIRONMENT BASED ON YOUR NEW DESIGNS. WHAT KIND OF EXPERIENCE DID YOU WISH TO BRING TO THE EVENT AND THE GUESTS?

First of all, a trade fair is a fairly busy and crowded environment in general. It was important to create a space that had a different look and feel and provided a strong spatial experience. Temporary VIP areas often tend to be designed to look permanent and extravagant, rather than to play on simplicity and creativity. The theme for the project was chosen to embrace the short-term conditions and was inspired by stage design and theatrical décor rather than traditional interior design. Furthermore, I sought to create a room-like feeling within the large space without using traditional walls or dividers. In the VIP area this was enabled using tree silhouettes cladded with balloons. Also, large clouds made of clusters

of oversized latex balloons were suspended from the ceiling absorbing noise and giving the area a surprisingly calm and relaxed feeling.

THE BAR DOUBLED AS A SOCIAL AND EXHIBITION AREA AT THE FAIR. HOW DID YOU COPE WITH ITS DUALITY? HAVE YOU COME ACROSS ANY DIFFICULTIES ALONG THE WAY?

The Design Bar project had two main objectives. Except being an appreciated place to relax and refuel at the busy fair, it served the purpose to promote young designers and the furniture fair itself. Visitors would be curious and expect something out of the ordinary; designing a functional space was just not enough. The project had gained a significant reputation in Scandinavia and become a springboard for emerging designers.

These conditions actually made it easier to engage the project. Except meeting functional needs such as a required number of seats, a dividing between VIP and public zones, security regulations, etc. the design had to stand out and provide a unique experience from the rest of the fair.

IF YOU HAVE ANOTHER CHANCE TO DESIGN A POP-UP EATERY, WHAT WOULD YOU LIKELY INCLUDE IN THE SETUP?

I appreciate and embrace the temporary, scenography look. This emphases that the setup aim to make an impression and the concept can be pushed further without feeling pretentious, but instead have a twinkle in the eye.

IS THERE SOMETHING ABOUT FOOD OR THE FOOD CULTURE THAT YOU WOULD BE EAGERLY EXPECTING TO SEE OR TASTE?

I like to see more strong thematic concepts that really push the envelope. Restaurants and bars are places where people stay for a couple of hours to experience something extraordinary. Half the experience is related to the physical space and includes light, sound and smell. The guest should be treated with a show, just like a visit to a theater or a concert.

NEON JELLY CHAMBER
Bompas & Parr

Glowing in jello blocks, these neon chambers are a site specific installation with a nod to Antonin Carême. Carême had gained fame for his great works of pastry and confectionary inspired by buildings and his 'haute cuisine' prepared for Napoleon, George IV and Tsar Alexander.

Photo / Ann Charlott Ommedal

ARTISANAL GUM FACTORY
Bompas & Parr

The world's first micro-factory has been built. Here, each visitor was allowed to experiment with composing gum flavours from 200 tangs including white truffle, tonic, curry and beer yeast. There were also gums that would change its flavour when chewed.

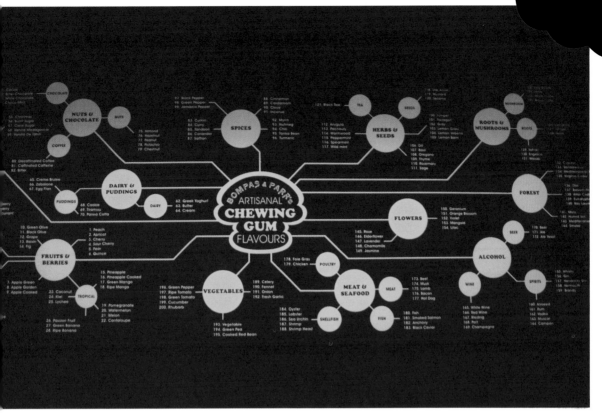

CURIOUS BREAKFAST
Paper Donut

Photo / Fanette Guilloud

Using paper as the mere ingredient of this home breakfast, *Curious Breakfast* is the essence of Paper Donut's curiosity, craftsmanship and imagination to kick off the day in the most French and American way.

ketchupy

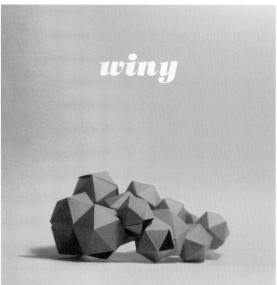
winy

crispy

juicy

PAPER FRUITS
Paper Donut

Photo / Fanette Guilloud

Like colours, fruits can be vivid connotations too. Playing on paper, volume and colours, *Paper Fruits* call up memories of taste, touch, texture and classic tales in a fruit basket with colour contrasts and words.

slightly

poisoned

silly

1

Photo / Leo Cackett

2

BURGERMATS
Burgerac

EVENT · EVENT

The Burgermat Show was born to celebrate burgers. Twenty-four artists were asked to create a new piece of art to adorn the placemats for the one-off Burger Monday event, where a three-course meal would be served, prepared by chef Fred Smith. Young & Foodish had co-organised the event.

1 / Nishant Choksi (Photo / Burgerac)
2 / Gemma Shiel
3 / Richard Hart
4 / Chrissie Macdonald, John Short

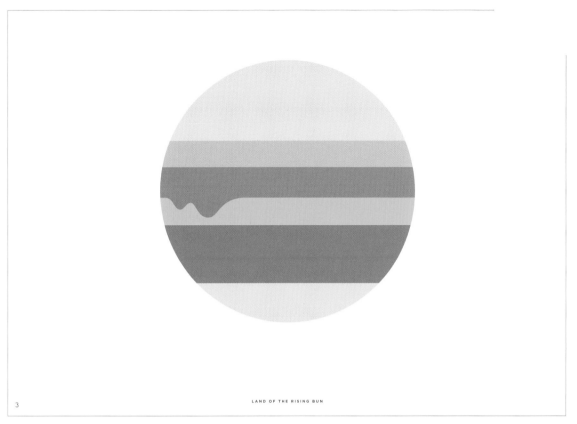

LAND OF THE RISING BUN

4

5

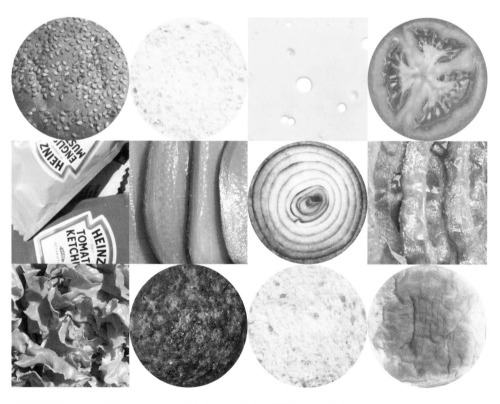

6

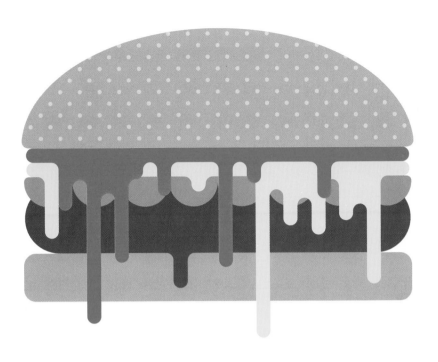

7

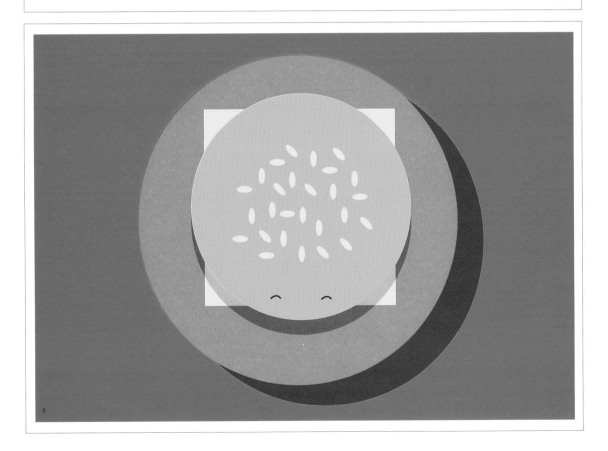

8

WHAT I ATE AT MN STATE FAIR
Brian Danaher

Danaher has created a pictorial record to recount the impressive variety of food he had
grobbled down at the Minnesota State Fair. Surprise, surprise — the food and drink tour was
inevitably concluded with two antacid tablets in the end.

hawaiian shaved ice   mini donuts   pop   grilled shrimp

pork chop   french fries   ice cream cone   water

fried cheese curds   beer   corn on the cob   cookies

chocolate malt   turkey sandwich   lemonade   antacid

★ ★ ★ **WHAT I ATE** *at the* **MN STATE FAIR** ★ ★ ★

FOOD OF THE RAINBOW
Henry Hargreaves

Styling / Lisa Edslav

Food of the Rainbow originated as a mother's trick to tempt her children. Wickedly artificial yet
edible, these real foods are restyled as a mash-up of the grotesque, beauty and curiosity to be
framed. The food is said to taste surprisingly normal despite its odd colours.

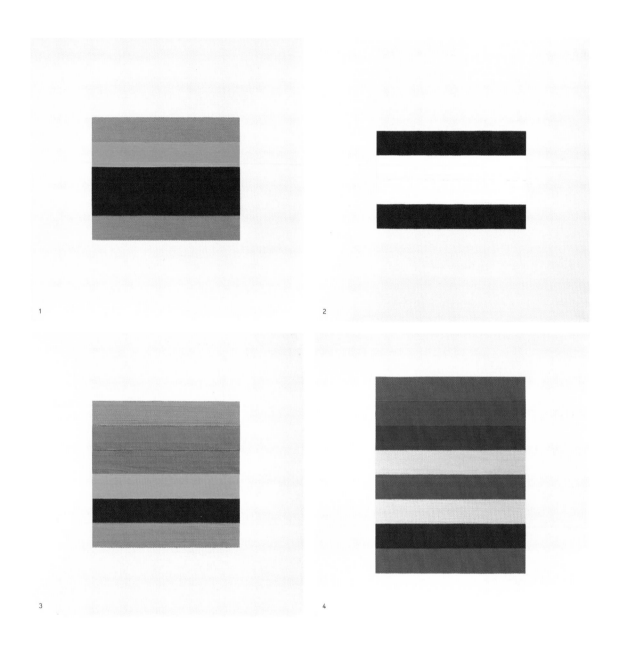

1

2

3

4

SANDWICHES
Dan Kenneally

Kenneally's acrylic painting collection depicts a range of abstracted sandwich recipes distilled to a stack of stripes in identical length and width but varied by colours and layers. The paintings are 18 inches by 18 inches in size.

1 / Cheesesteak
2 / Ice Cream Sandwich
3 / Cheeseburger
4 / Giordano Bros. Sandwich
5 / Cream Cheese & Lox
6 / Reuben
7 / Bacon Egg & Cheese
8 / Peanut Butter & Jelly

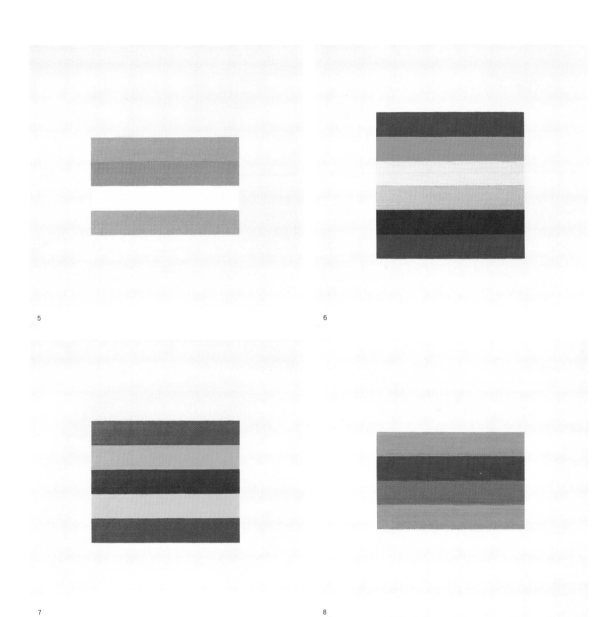

5

6

7

8

SWEET VEGGIES
Wendy van Santen

Thanks to photographer Wendy van Santen and art director Hans Bolleurs, broccoli, peas and leeks can now be called 'confections' too. Visually charming, these stills of decorated plants work a treat on bringing fantasy to real life.

Photo / Richard Gilligan

1 / Ben Newman
2 / Celestine Cooney
3 / DALEK
4 / BrenB
5 / Rilla Alexander
6 / SHOE
7 / Linda Brownlee
8 / Mario Sughi
9 / Steve Alexander
10 / The London Police

ABSOLUT VIS10NS
The Small Print

As part of ABSOLUT Fringe 2011, THE SMALL PRINT has enrolled a host of artists from various creative disciplines across the globe to customise ten life-size ABSOLUT bottles within a week. These giant creations were later put on public's view at Dublin's South Studios.

1

DIE OUT
Timothy Berg and Rebekah Myers

Berg and Myer's recent work revolves around notions of cultural consumption. Depicting popular desserts diminishing at different phases, these projects prompt viewers to interpret "disappear-ance" and rethink the consequences behind the joy of consumption with no limits.

Photo / John Lucas
1 / Here today, gone tomorrow
2 / Enjoy it... while it lasts
3 / Something for nothing

Photo / Timothy Berg and Rebekah Myers
4 / Get 'em fore' they're gone

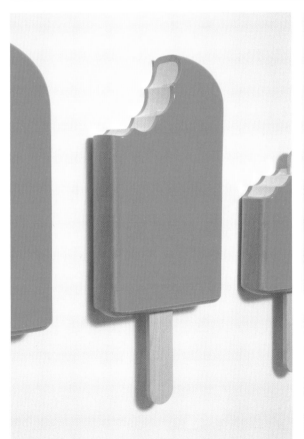

2

4

SOCIAL KITCHEN
Alt Group

Furniture / Sam Haughton (IMO), Fisher & Paykel
Special Credits / Pradeep Sharma, Toaki Okano

Fisher & Paykel's has manifested their design philosophy in *Social Kitchen*, which suggests the new role of modern kitchens as social hubs, surrounded by New Zealand's best appliance engineering and designs. Visitors were treated to a range of bite-sized works of art created by Engine Room.

FARINA
Glasfurd & Walker

Interior / Craig Stanghetta

Farina is a self-serviced pizzeria meant to inspire a sense of community. Like its food concept, the overall design is simple and sleek. Its housemade artisan products, such as raw tomato sauce and Oregano-infused olive oil, are particularly highlighted and displayed as decor in the store.

TOMATO SAUCE
PIZZERIA FARINA
pizzeriafarina.com   16oz

OREGANO INFUSED OLIVE OIL

CHILI INFUSED OLIVE OIL
pizzeriafarina.com

! NELLA VITA –
CHI NON RISICA –
NON ROSICA

PIZZERIA FARINA

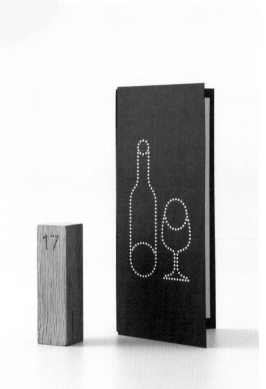

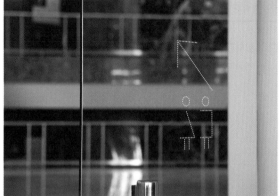
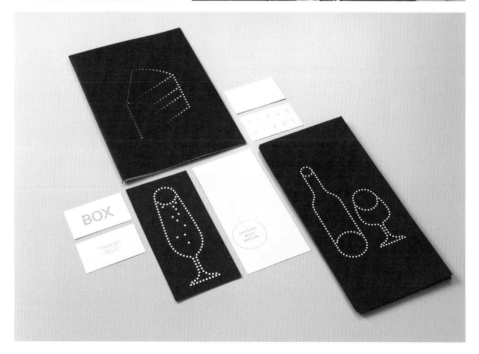

BOX CAFÉ
Alt Group

The name tells it all – Box Café is a ticket office, a bar, a lunch destination, as well as a space for
private events. The dotted solution in its logomark has borrowed ideas from the design vernacular
of theatre lighting, dot matrix printers and perforations on admission ticket boards.

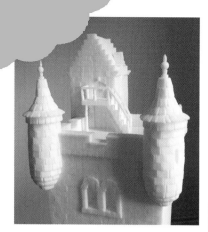

HELEN'S TOWER
Brendan Jamison

Jamison has taken inspirations from 19th Century Scottish architect William Burn's Helen's Tower and crafted his own version out of white sugar cubes. Solid yet feminine, the sugar replica exhibits Jamison's craftsmanship through its delicate details, such as the turrets and staircase at the top.

TATE MODERN & NEO BANKSIDE
Brendan Jamison

Built to the scale of 1:100, *Tate Modern & NEO Bankside* is an imaginative contribution to London Festival of Architecture. The sugar sculptures were commissioned by CAMRON and Native Land and Grosvenor. NEO Bankside is designed by Rogers Stirk Harbour + Partners.

CAFÉ/DAY
Suppose Design Office

Started without a name, Café/day has established itself as a truely open 'izakaya' after division walls are taken down and its surrounding features taking over its interior. Other features like car seats, bus stop bench and road markings were added to intensify the feel.

T-MAGI
We Architecture

Photo / Enok Holsegaard

As Mariage Frères' retailer in Copenhagen, T-magi features a giant teapot picked out on backlit perforations as a powerful eye-catcher at the storefront. Visually clean and bright like a lab, the store invites customers to taste and smell the teas displayed across the scent wall.

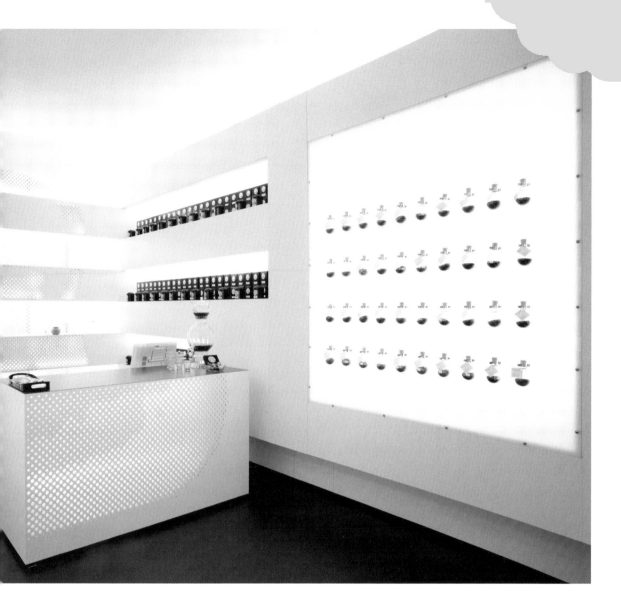

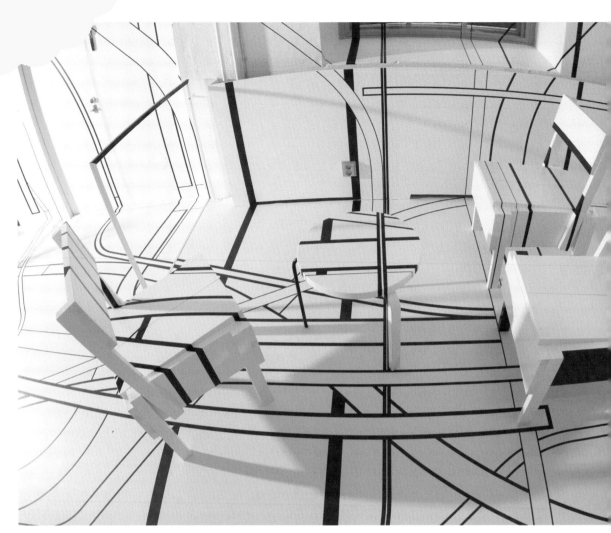

LOGOMO CAFÉ
Artek oy ab, Tobias Rehberger

Photo / Bo Stranden

Tobias Rehberger's created a piece of spatial art for Logomo Café, titled *Nothing Happens For A Reason*. The graphic environment has aimed to transport visitors to a total visual experience as part of the European Capital of Culture 2011. The project was completed with furniture sponsored by Artek.

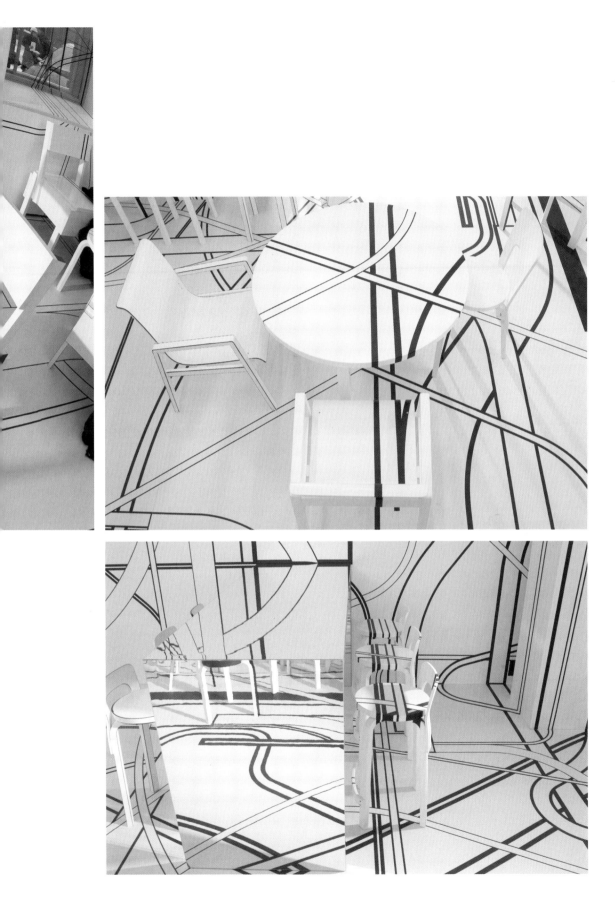

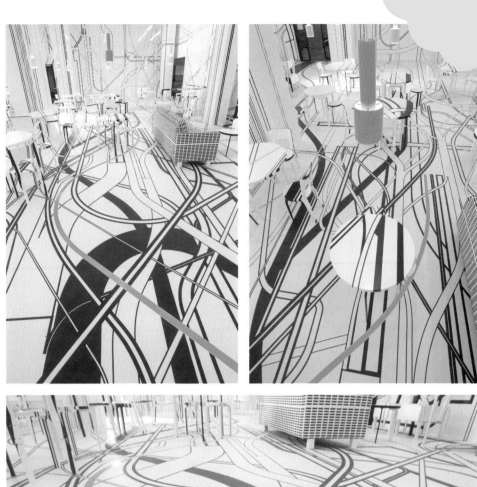

THE HATCH
Studio Toogood

Photo / Tom Mannion

Named 'The Hatch', the architectural eatery was opened to serve egg-inspired recipe kits at London Design Festival 2009. Daubed with handpainted Hockneyesque patterns next to a stack of mini building blocks, the venue was set to resurrect everyone's childlike desire to relax and create.

THE SALAD SHOP
Asylum

Photo / Edwin Tan (Lumina Photography Singapore)

"Salad for Everybody" is integral to The Salad Shop's brand philosophy. Greeting passers-by with a glimpse of the interior via a massive cutouts of forks and spoons, the interior offers a breath of nature enriched by animal graphics, installations and a texture mix.

BIOGRAPHY

AbelPartners Design Studio
▶ P.118-119 ▶ ▶

Co-founded in 2008 by brand manager, Jung-Joo Kwon and product designer, Sung-Mun Yoon, in Seoul, Korea. By instilling creative concepts and ideas into every piece of work, their products are distributed locally and in the overseas. AbelPartners also attends to various design exhibitions such as Maison & Object 2010 in Paris and Designboom Mart 2011 in New York.

Access Agency
▶ P.138-139 ▶ ▶

A global creative agency commited to designing extraordinary creative experiences that inspire consumers through compelling communication.

Alt Group
▶ P.222-225, 228-229 ▶ ▶ ▶

Based in Auckland, New Zealand, Alt Group is a multidisciplinary design studio founded in 2000 by Ben Corban and Dean Poole. Now a core team of 20 people with diversified backgrounds and experiences in design, business, brand strategy, communication design, interactive design and new product development, the company has been recognised in numerous international awards including ADC, AIGA, AGDA, Cannes Lions, The One Show, Red Dot and TDC.

Anagrama
▶ P.134-137 ▶ ▶ ▶

Specialised in brand development and positioning providing creative solutions for any type of project, Anagrama is also expertised in the design and development of objects, spaces and multimedia projects. With attention to the smallest of details, the business consultancy provides solutions based on the analysis of tangible data to generate best-fit applications.

Après Ski
▶ P.022-023 ▶ ▶ ▶

Lucía Vergara's line of accessories. The designer is based in Barcelona, Spain who, after working for Lydia Delgado and Ailanto, launched her own collection in 2009. It is a brand that identifies itself original, special and unique with most of its pieces made of old materials from the 40s to the 80s. The inspiration for Après Ski focuses mainly on the fauna and flora of the nature, on geometric designs and on the universe.

Artek oy ab
▶ P.240-243 ▶ ▶ ▶

Founded in 1935 by four young idealists, Alvar and Aino Aalto, Maire Gullichsen and Nils-Gustav Hahl, Artek's business idea was "to sell furniture and to promote a modern culture of habitation by exhibitions and other educational means." The founders advocated a new kind of environment for everyday life with a grand synthesis of the arts and they wanted to make a difference in town planning as well as architecture and design.

Today Artek is renowned as being one of the most innovative contributors to modern design. Functionality and timeless aesthetics are the essential elements in the creation of every of their products.

Asylum
▶ P.246-249 ▶ ▶ ▶

Founded in 1999 as a creative company that comprises of a design studio, a retail store, a workshop and a record label. Since its inception in 1999, Asylum has worked on crossdisciplinary projects that includes interactive design, product development, environmental and interior design, package design, apparel design, branding and graphic design. Asylum won more than 70 international awards including The One Show and D&AD. In 2008, the studio was also quoted "probably the best design agency in Singapore today" by ICON (UK).

At Pace
▶ P.063 ▶ ▶ ▶

Situated in the heart of Claremont, Cape Town, At Pace is a design and advertising company made up of a handpicked team of communication specialists including designers, writers and production managers. They produce package design, corporate identities and print collaterals for some of the country's biggest brands, including SABMiller, Johnson & Johnson and Parmalat. They also design for some of the finest wine estates in the Cape.

Atipus
▶ P.050-051 ▶ ▶ ▶

Established in Barcelona since 1998, Atipus is a design studio providing graphic design and web services for companies, associations and public institutions. Their work includes corporate projects, product lines, brands, campaigns, congresses, events, etc.

Based on personal attention to clients' specific needs throughout each project, Atipus' team has established satisfactory long-term relationships with a large number of clients.

Bean, Kyle
▶ P.168 ▶ ▶ ▶

An artist and designer specialising in handmade models, set design and tactile illustration, Bean actually graduated in illustration from the University of Brighton in 2009. He has worked for a diverse range of clients across a number of platforms such as creating window displays for luxury brands including Liberty, Selfridges and Hermès, and editorial commissions for publications like Wallpaper, Financial Times, VMAN and Wired. Alongside his commercial work, Bean has produced some personal projects that have gained him international recognition. He has exhibited his work in London and at the International Design Biennial in St. Etienne, France.

BERG
▶ P.142 ▶ ▶ ▶

An independent UK based ideas studio. Design seamlessly across a wide range of interdisciplinary media including prints, screen and the environment, BERG has an international reputation for consistently applying innovation, imagination, and sound commercial values. The team works closely with clients and industry professionals to create solutions that are considered, engaging and effective.

Bettina Nissen Design
▶ P.020-021 ▶ ▶ ▶

With an eye for observation and the ability to extract everyday symbols and routines, then incorporating them into designs, Nissen works to feature contrasting elements or materials in her work creating curious, thoughtful and witty contemporary design. These include furniture, home accessories, lighting and jewelry. Fusing simple but functional forms with humour, Nissen utilises new technology creating innovative products that generate subtle shifts in common perception of daily life.

Boffoli, Christopher
▶ P.170-181 ▶ ▶ ▶

A writer, journalist, photographer, filmmaker and artist, Boffoli's work has appeared online and in print publications in more than 60 countries around the world. He is currently based in Seattle, Washington, USA.

Bompas & Parr
▶ P.193-195 ▶ ▶ ▶

Named by the Independent magazine as one of "The 15 people who will define the future of arts in Britain", Bompas & Parr designs spectacular experiences often on an architectural scale with cutting edge technology. Founded by Sam Bompas and Harry Parr in 2007, the studio has slowly grown to its current structure of about 10 people, generating a wide range of projects and collaborating with various curators, cultural practitioners, and scientists.

Burgerac
▶ P.200-203 ▶▶▶

The result of a 2011 new year will to eat more burgers, Burgerac started the blog about great burgers made with freshly prepared (never frozen) meat patties of coarsley ground beef with an 80/20 lean meat to fat ratio, cooked to a perfect medium rare, and presented in a soft white bun. Burgerac believes that burgers, with a carefully considered and balanced blend of flavours and textures, have the potential to delight senses like any other great culinary dish.

www.burgermat.com

Chocolate Editions by Mary & Matt
▶ P.032-033 ▶▶▶

Mary Matson and Matt Even met in high school and began a lifelong artistic collaboration. While studying painting, the duo developed the love for design, food and culinary arts. Matson worked in design and pastry, Even in advertising. They then began to make things that they found missing in their life. Matson and Even believe in modernism with a smile.

CoDesign Ltd.
▶ P.056-057 ▶▶▶

Co-founded by Eddy Yu and Hung Lam in 2003, CoDesign specialises in branding and corporate identity, environmental graphics, literature and packaging design. Characterised by simple and effective design with bold and innovative concepts, CoDesign has earned the trust from many major corporations and institutions in Hong Kong. The establishment of CoLab in recent years has enabled CoDesign using design as an intermediary to integrate the commercial world, the arts and society.

Cornwell
▶ P.146-149 ▶▶▶

Founded in 1993 by Steven Cornwell and Jane Sinclair, Cornwell is recognised by the industry as a premier Australian brand and communications agency. The award-winning studio of 30 strategy, design and account service professionals brings an insightful and strategic focus to brand-oriented business issues. In 2004, Cornwell joined the STW Group, Australia's largest communications services group to further strengthen its depth of services. 16 years since the company's inception, the brand continues to thrive and attract clients that demand a high level of strategic thinking and creative execution.

Couple
▶ P.150-151 ▶▶▶

Founded in 2007 by two designers, Couple encompasses a broad scope of design activities including printed matters, moving images, exhibitions, urban spaces, and corporate branding and communications.

Creamer, Alex
▶ P.094 ▶▶▶

Studied graphic design at the University of Central Lancashire and graduated in 2011, Creamer had a years' industrial placement in London working at The Partners, Honey Creative, Ziggurat Brands and Landor Associates a year before.

Creasence
▶ P.095 ▶▶▶

Established in the Czech Republic in 2006, Creasence is an independent group of experts in the sphere of visual and interactive design, UI design and websites building. The team has 10-year experience in the field and is recognised by world-known companies.

Danaher, Brian
▶ P.204-205 ▶▶▶

An art director, designer, illustrator, chronic doodler, coffee drinker and music addict based in the mid-west of the United States.

Depot WPF
▶ P.058-059 ▶▶▶

Based in Russia providing integrated solutions on brand positioning, corporate visual identity and communicative strategy, Depot WPF's worldwide clients include Nestle, Unilever, DANONE, Philips, Campbells, Kimberly Clark, etc. Founded in 1998, it is today one of the biggest agencies with about 50 people in staff. It has been repeatedly ranked as Russia's most creative agency according to the ACAR rating and a frequent winner of numerous awards like Cannes Lions 2011, The Dieline 2011, Cresta Awards 2011, Epica Awards, Golden Drum, Golden Hammer, ADCR Awards, and many more.

DEUTSCHE & JAPANER Creative Studio
▶ P.144-145 ▶▶▶

Initiated in 2008 offering expertise in various disciplines like graphic design, product design, interior design, illustration and scenography as well as conceptual creation and strategic brand escort, the studio focuses on communication and is always in regard of sustainable experiences.

Fraile, Eduardo del
▶ P.010-011, 061 ▶▶▶

With a 3.80m high studio in an antique building in Spain, Fraile has been working for companies in various countries for over a decade. His work spans from packaging, identity and editorial design. The designer and art director also speaks at conferences from time to time. He has received more than 80 international awards and has been a frequent jury in various international prizes. In April 2010, he formed part of the packaging jury for D&AD in London.

Gauthier Designers
▶ P.090-091 ▶▶▶

Founded in 1987, Gauthier Designers is a communication and design firm based in Montreal, Canada. Known for its strategic approach, the firm has gained a solid reputation for quality. Strategic mindedness and a penchant for clarity, Gauthier colours its creative process with incisive results. Made up of passionate people, Gauthier thrives on straightforwardness.

Glasfurd & Walker
▶ P.158-161, 226-227 ▶▶▶

Formed by Australian designer Phoebe Glasfurd and Canadian producer Aren Fieldwalker in early 2007, Glasfurd & Walker is a creative studio specialising in ideation, graphic design and artistic direction for print and online communication, exhibition, installation and packaging. Strategic and idea-driven design is the constant in their approach that brings in functional and aesthetic necessities. The duo believes that design plays an important role in business success and the world we live in, and it should always be as considered, effective and beautiful as possible.

HAF
▶ P.105 ▶▶▶

A company manufacturing and distributing alternative lifestyle design products. Based in Reykjavik, Iceland, HAF was founded by industrial and interior designer Hafsteinn Juliusson in 2011.

Juliusson likes to approach design from new perspectives and reach a diverse range of people. He always gets involved with society, ecology and try to avoid mainstream mass production. Juliusson experiments on a broad forum, he is fascinated by simple things with fun solutions which have a rich and strong concept.

HAMILTON TURKSOY
▶ P.116-117 ▶▶▶

The creative partnership of Kacper Hamilton and Ezgi Turksoy. They met whilst studying together at Central Saint Martins, London. The studio was founded in 2009 and is based in London where they work on a variety of projects from glass to furniture design. Their work is primarily based on the emotional relationship formed between objects and users. The duo explores how experience and stories can be formed by interacting with objects in everyday life. Their individual and collaborative work has been widely published and exhibited in books, magazines and galleries around the world.

Hargreaves, Henry

▶ P.206-207 ▶ ▶ ▶

The photographer's introduction to this industry began in front of the camera. He was the pin-up boy for revered fashion houses like Prada, YSL, Jil Sander, Lacoste, etc. and worked with the top photographers in the field. Hargreaves settled in New York sometime around 2008 and opened a studio in Brooklyn. He has been shooting full time ever since, specialising in both still life and fashion photography. His clients include Ralph Lauren, NY Magazine, GQ, NYLON, Boucheron, Marie Claire, Gilt Groupe, Christies, I.D., Edun and many more.

Harris, Jesse

▶ P.156-157 ▶ ▶ ▶

A recent graduate from the Edinburgh College of Art with an obsession for innovative and original food and drink packaging, Harris spent the fourth and final year developing the brand identity, visuals and packaging for a fictional fishmongers based in Stockbridge Edinburgh.

Hayashi, Atsuhiro

▶ P.014 ▶ ▶ ▶

Born in Kyoto and graduated from Kyoto Seika University in 1989, Hayashi is now working as a freelance product designer in Osaka, Japan.

Hill, Demelza

▶ P.019 ▶ ▶ ▶

Based in London, Hill's design based around people's perceptions and reactions to materials, forms and objects. Through a wide variety of work including accessories, lighting, furniture and sculpture, Hill uses familiar forms and interactions to evolve people's impression for the materials or functions of everyday objects, allowing end-users to envisage beyond their normal boundaries. Hill has started up her own studio in 2011.

imm Living

▶ P.089 ▶ ▶ ▶

A Toronto-based design company that addresses notions of the past and present. Drawing from the traditional and popular cultures of the world, imm Living creates designs marrying functionality with a playful sensibility. As varied as the people behind each project, their work is injected with rich meaning, evoking emotion between objects and people, while bridging cultural differences. imm Living gives a voice to these everyday functional objects, creating stories that empower the need for significance.

Imre, Eszter

▶ P.078-087 ▶ ▶ ▶

Born 1985 in Hungary, Imre graduated in Master of Fine Arts specialising in ceramics in 2010. Living in Sweden and working within different fields, techniques and all over places, Imre always describes herself as "curious, precise, and independent." She often looks for different fields and techniques that can let her play around. Among all materials, porcelain is what Imre knows best and works mostly with.

Inhouse Design

▶ P.060 ▶ ▶ ▶

A boutique design studio of Arch and Jane MacDonnell based in Auckland, New Zealand. Established in 1995, Inhouse Design's niche is best described as high-end with a skew toward arts and culture. The studio prides itself on producing beautifully crafted design that is simple, effective and appropriate to every one of its clients.

Jamison, Brendan

▶ P.230-231 ▶ ▶ ▶

Born 1979 in Belfast, Northern Ireland, Jamison studied at the University of Ulster, gaining his MFA in 2004. He has exhibited globally over the past seven years.

In 2009 a small work of his was entered into the permanent collection of MOMA New York, being part of the project titled 'A Book About Death'.

In 2010, Jamison was commissioned to build sugar cube scale models of Tate Modern and NEO Bankside for the London Festival of Architecture. Afterwards, his sugar sculptures were sold at Sotheby's, Bond Street, London. He is represented by the Golden Thread Gallery, Dickon Hall Ltd. and Nixon Art.

Jasmin Schuller || Visual Entertainment

▶ P.044-047 ▶ ▶ ▶

Born and raised in Graz, Austria, Schuller quit her occupation as a graphic designer in 2007 and turned her long-term passion for photography to profession. Central to humankind and surroundings, Schuller's work breaks the mold of aesthetic bias with a sharp look at social conventions. The photographer likes to move people with her work and to get people to smile with her subtle sense of irony.

Jonas Wagell Design & Architecture

▶ P.188-192 ▶ ▶ ▶

A Swedish architect and designer located in Stockholm, Wagell is trained in graphics, marketing, design and architecture at institutions such as Konstfack, Beckmans, Berghs and Parsons and has a back record in strategic project management. In 2008, Wagell was named one of "the World's 50 hottest young architects" by Wallpaper magazine and his prefab house concept, Mini House received the Innovation Award from the Swedish Chamber of Commerce in London.

Kabiljo Inc.

▶ P.164-165 ▶ ▶ ▶

A Viennese brand designing and producing objects with little fetishes, bad habits and compulsive actions. Their products search for innovation on the level of human behaviour. Materials are carefully researched and subdued to series of experimental processes until they fit into place. To Kabiljo Inc., fantasy is bent around tough materials and simple things are created for complex times, nice, irony-free and celebratory.

KaCaMa Design Lab

▶ P.107 ▶ ▶ ▶

A group of Hong Kong-based product designers who specialise in reusing post-consumer waste materials. With various backgrounds in product design, packaging and eco-design, KaCaMa's products not only delight people's lives and instill eco-awareness in its users, but also establish contacts with local enterprises, handcraft men and local cultures.

Kaneuchi, Yukihiro

▶ P.127 ▶ ▶ ▶

Bored 1984 in Fukuoka, Japan, Kaneuchi graduated in Art and Architecture at the Tama Art University in Tokyo. The designer was the winner of Cumulous Kyoto 2008, International Design Competition in 2008 and granted with a researcher scholarship at Fabrica, Italy in 2009.

Kaynak, Burak

▶ P.102-103 ▶ ▶ ▶

Born in Istanbul, Turkey, Kaynak now lives in Montreal, Canada. He always says, "If I'm not surprising myself, no wonder I'm boring you!"

Kenneally, Dan

▶ P.208-209 ▶ ▶ ▶

Born and raised in New York, Kenneally picked up design after he failed his pro basketball dreams joining the high school basketball team. A graduate of the School of Visual Arts in New York, Kenneally works an art director in advertising as well as his personal art projects.

Kinetic Singapore

▶ P.152-155 ▶ ▶ ▶

Grown to become one of the Singapore's foremost creative shops, Kinetic was founded in 1999 as an interactive agency. The additonal design and advertising arm set up in 2001 providing a full range of integrated marketing solutions has allowed the agency to break new and substantial ground in its work. It has won several international and local advertising awards including Cannes Lions, the British D&AD, the One Show in the United States and the Young Guns in Australia. Kinetic has always garnered top awards and shown its mettle.

Klausner, Judith
▶ P.106 ▶ ▶ ▶

A Somerville MA artist with a love for small, intricate, and overlooked things, Klausner received her degree in studio art from the Wesleyan University in 2007. After constructing her thesis primarily out of insects, Klausner has since continued to search the details of her surroundings for inspiration. She enjoys playing with her food, both recreationally and professionally.

Kleiner, Carl & Kleiner, Evelina
▶ P.028-031 ▶ ▶ ▶

Virtually self-taught, Kleiner quit art school after only one year of study and he assisted for a short period before beginning to take on commissions himself. Kleiner works closely with his set designer and wife Evelina Bratell. The imagery they create is the result of a careful interplay between varying elements, often to comic effect. Kleiner looks to reveal the personality of the objects he photographs yet his unique compositions take on a personality of their own. They are imaginative, droll and absurd in equal measure with a sense of fragility. The husband-and-wife team lives and works in Stockholm.

Korefe
▶ P.008-009, 016-017, 048-049, 093, 096-099 ▶ ▶ ▶

The integrated design and innovations agency of Kolle Rebbe. Ranked one of the Germany's most awarded design agencies, Korefe is specialised in corporate design, corporate publishing, packaging and product development. Korefe covers the entire spectrum and process of innovation from market analysis to naming and design.

Laikingland
▶ P.015 ▶ ▶ ▶

Based in the UK and The Netherlands, Laikingland designs and manufactures kinetic objects that engage and evoke a sense of play and nostalgia. Founded in 2008 upon a life long friendship between artist, Martin Smith and engineer, Nick Regan, Laikingland has specialised in producing highly crafted limited editions, working closely with invited artists and designers to realise their kinetic ideas. Alongside their products, Laikingland also regularly carries out projects to create one-off, special edition and exclusive kinetic objects and displays.

Logerot, Aïssa
▶ P.120 ▶ ▶ ▶

Studied cabinetmaking formation at Ecole Boulle and graduated at Ensci, Logerot creates objects with essential lines that respond to a functional aesthetic and to a reasoned use of materials. His work raises questions on eco-design and the links between design and art craft. The winner of the Reddot Award 2009 before being nominated for the Audi Talents Awards, Logerot also won the Cinna competition 2010 and recently awarded the Grand Prize for Creation of the City of Paris 2010.

Ludvig Bruneau Rossow
▶ P.162-163 ▶ ▶ ▶

The studio of Ludvig Bruneau Rossow, a graphic designer based in Oslo, Norway. Work mainly with prints, from visual identities to editorial design and packaging, Rossow believes that design should have a function and not just appears as decoration. The ideas behind his projects vary from technical to emotional concepts.

MAEZM
▶ P.128-129 ▶ ▶ ▶

The design studio of EunWhan Cho and TaiHo Shin, MAEZM works on various fields including lighting design, furniture, space, and architectural design based on endless tests of differences among objects. Their work is introduced at numerous domestic and foreign exhibitions and won several awards.

Masahiro Minami Laboratory
▶ P.140-141 ▶ ▶ ▶

Born 1978 in Osaka, Japan, Minami was a research associate in the Department of Living Design at the University of Shiga Prefecture in 2005. He established the Masahiro Minami Laboratory the same year and then Masahiro Minami Design in 2008. In 2011, he becomes an assistant professor to the Department of Living Design at the same university.

MENOSUNOCEROUNO
▶ P.143 ▶ ▶ ▶

An advertising agency, a branding boutique, an editorial house, and a digital agency designed as a "one stop shop" based on business, strategy, creativity and design, MENOSUNOCEROUNO translates clients business strategy into mobilising communication strategies with simple yet powerful stories connecting people with brands and brands with people. The agency believes that brands should always smell, taste, feel, sound, look, speak and behave in a way that is unforgettable. Since 2001 of its inception, their work is recognised for its powerful simplicity and surgical aesthetic.

Method
▶ P.053 ▶ ▶ ▶

With offices in the United States and Europe, Method is an international design firm focused on product and service innovation. Leading by Robert Murdock, the Chief Creative Officer of the firm, the team solves business challenges through design thinking creating inspired products, services and experiences. Their user-centric design approach has built great experiences across touch points and through customer lifecycles. Method is an independent unit of GlobalLogic as well as a leader in the field of software research and development services.

Mika, Tsutai
▶ P.110-111 ▶ ▶ ▶

Born 1988 in Japan, Mika graduated in design at Kyoto Institute of Technology in 2011. Mika won several awards like the JIN's Eyewear Design Contest 2008, IRIS Daily Goods Design Competition 2009 and the Judge's Special Prize of Tokyo Midtown Award 2010 during his studies. Mika has two solo exhibitions in his graduation year.

Mint
▶ P.064 ▶ ▶ ▶

A design consultancy opened in 2010 by designers Maja Matas and Kresimir Miloloza. Based in Zagreb, Croatia, Mint works across the fields of visual communication design, industrial design, advertising and design consulting. The young designers from Mint are also constantly participating in international exhibitions, workshops and competitions.

Morales, Linus
▶ P.038-039 ▶ ▶ ▶

Born and raised in the very south of Sweden, Morales is influenced by his father who was also a photographer, and found his interest in photography in a very young age. After two years of photography study in Sweden, he had an internship in New York and started out as an assistant to beauty and fashion photographer Iain Crawford in London. Currently based in London and Sweden, Morales mainly shoots for fashion and art with a passion to combine both in a graphic way and he likes to capture the natural moment in a more documentary way.

Moving Brands
▶ P.114-115 ▶ ▶ ▶

An independent, award-winning branding consultant with offices in London, Zurich, Tokyo and San Francisco. Through unique approach to brand strategy, brand identity and brand experience, the creative studios create powerful new ways for brands to connect with people, and people to connect with brands. Their aim is to redefine branding by setting new standards of creativity for a moving world.

Nelson Associates
▶ P.062 ▶ ▶ ▶

A Surrey-based design studio founded by creative director Christian Nelson. With a reputation of creating thoughtful, considered, beautifully produced design, Nelson Associates works with clients and brands that seek to present themselves in a way which is both distinctive and memorable. Working closely with a network of award-winning collaborators the studio is able to draw together the right team to create work that is relevant, powerful and commercially effective for each and every client.

NOSIGNER
▶ P.092 ▶ ▶ ▶

A design and innovation firm that re-envision brands with essential experiences. The team works within the fields of products, graphics, art, communication, space, and architecture. NOSIGNER believes that design can solve social problems. By creating fresh design experiences, they work with sustainability, education, isolated locality, disaster restoration, and break stereotypes.

Ohmine Shuzou Co., Ltd
▶ P.054-055 ▶ ▶ ▶

Ohmine Shuzou has run its cellar and brewed sake since the 17th century. Launched in 2010, "Ohmine" starts as a small-scale production in 5,000 liters a year by a group of people harbouring the hope to "brew a sake that overthrows conventions and weaves in an international perspective". While preserving the traditions inherited from the predecessors, Ohmine Shuzou aims to present cutting edge ideas without being bound by customs and bring the "Ohmine" brand to the world.

Paper Donut
▶ P.196-199 ▶ ▶ ▶

Founded in 2009 by Alexis Facca who realised the potential of geometrical handmade paper work for corporate, the French paper collective has worked a lot with IF Magazine and collaborated with various artists like Justine Ricaud, Fanette Guilloud, and Benoît.

Pedrita
▶ P.052 ▶ ▶ ▶

The design studio of Rita João and Pedro Ferreira. Met during their studies, João studied at TU Delft and Ferreira at Politecnico di Milano. They joined Fabrica in 2002 and led its 3D Design Department in 2004. Returning to Lisbon in 2005, the duo founded the studio and has since collaborated with creative units and clients worldwide like TAP Portugal, Camper, EXD, and Amop. Inspired by Portuguese traditional forms and techniques, Pedrita's work casts an inquisitive look on material culture in projects that are candid and quietly eloquent.

PEGA D&E
▶ P.012-013 ▶ ▶ ▶

A design consultancy that provides creative solutions in industrial design. Established in 2008 with offices in Taipei, Shanghai and Beijing, PEGA

D&E is part of a nearly decade-long tradition of hard work and exceptional design. It was part of the award-winning ASUS design team before becoming an independent consultancy, with their expertise applied in the consumer electronic world to diverse industries.

Peter Ibruegger
▶ P.122-125 ▶ ▶ ▶

Based in London working as an independent designer, Ibruegger created the DALIAN brand in 2009. Initially launched in Paris and London, it became an instant success and is frequently featured by major international publications and stocked worldwide.

Point-Blank Design Ltd.
▶ P.034-035 ▶ ▶ ▶

Founded by Lawrence Choy in 1996, the studio provides end-to-end design solutions, from brand identity to spatial design. The team believes that brand building is a sophisticated matter of structuring visible and intangible elements, accentuating the functionality and human dimension of a product or a service with unsurpassed creativity. Specific means and materials are applied to distinguish a brand in a design context that delivers clarity and lucidity, all along taking clients' needs into account.

Rafael Morgan Studio
▶ P.112-113 ▶ ▶ ▶

Born 1983 in Brazil, Morgan was raised in Belo Horizonte, means beautiful horizon, in Brazil that provides the designer endless inspirations. Started as an industrial designer, Morgan believes that good design must tell a story or at least makes people smile. The studio, set up upon the designer's graduation, works for various companies around the world. It also has a strategic partnership with Studio Mango, a Dutch design studio.

Ryohei Yoshiyuki to job
▶ P.100-101 ▶ ▶ ▶

The Japanese designer believes that finding and doing experiments is "a bit more" than ordinary in daily life. He works with several clients and also produces personal collections. The studio is set up in 2008 in the Netherlands.

Sander Lucas Ontwerpen
▶ P.182-187 ▶ ▶ ▶

Characterised by the new perspective on exciting interior products, Lucas creates new functionality and esthetic quality through adjusting, adding and combining.

Santen, Wendy van
▶ P.210-211 ▶ ▶ ▶

A photographer based in Amsterdam, the Netherlands, Santen is a perfectionist who loves to carefully construct her still series in the studio. Her work can be recognised by its minimal composition and conceptual message. Santen works to create images that surprise people and inspire them to look at the world in a different way.

Savvy Studio
▶ P.066-077 ▶ ▶ ▶

A multidisciplinary studio dedicated to developing brand experiences that generate emotions between clients and target audience, Savvy Studio approaches every project with a comprehensive and open creative process, which facilitates the participation of their clients in every step. Composed of specialists in the areas of marketing, communication, graphic design, industrial design, creative copywriting and architecture, the team also collaborates with talented artists and designers worldwide, allowing them to offer creative and innovative solutions with a global competitive edge.

Sebastian Bergne Ltd
▶ P.109 ▶ ▶ ▶

Based in London, Bergne set up the studio after graduating from The Royal College of Art in 1990. He has collaborated with well-known manufacturers including Authentics, Tefal, MUJI, Habitat, De Beers, Moulinex, Gaia & Gino and Vitra. His work shows less of a signature style but more a quest for appropriate new solutions to diverse design problems, whether working on bespoke projects or anonymous consumer products. Widely recognised with international design awards, frequent publications, exhibitions and inclusions in permanent collections such as The Museum of Modern Art, New York and the Design Museum, London, Bergne also carries guest speaking, lecturing and jury participation.

Studio Toogood
▶ P.244-245 ▶ ▶ ▶

Designs, directs and executes interiors and environments from concept through to creation, the studio's projects range from the two-dimensional page to the three-dimensional space.

Creative directed by Faye Toogood, the team consists of a wide range of talents in diverse backgrounds including fine art, art history, architecture and interior design. The studio collaborates with clients who seek alternative ways of developing their brand or their interior. Its distinctive approach disregards convention in favour of something altogether more brave, joyous and impulsive.

StudioKahn
▶ P.130-133 ▶ ▶ ▶

Founded in 2009 by Mey and Boaz Kahn who graduated in product design at Bezalel Academy, the studio designs, develops and manufactures products that lay on the borderline between industrial products and conceptual objects. Made mainly of casted ceramic, their works are characterised by clean forms with cultural and social statements. StudioKahn's products have been recognised, publicised and exhibited worldwide and won several design awards. The duo is based in Jerusalem, Israel.

studioooij
▶ P.126 ▶ ▶ ▶

The studio of the Dutch product designer, Marianne van Ooij who tells stories through her design. Her work always challenges its own function and the common perception about a product.

Founded in Brooklyn in 2009, studioooij works in a variety of disciplines including textiles, furniture and ceramics. Clients include The Metropolitan Opera in New York and Present Time in the Netherlands. Ooij's work has received global attention, most recently from the New York Times and Abitare, Italy.

Suppose Design Office
▶ P.232-235 ▶ ▶ ▶

The studio of Makoto Tanijiri. Born 1974 in Hiroshima, Japan the architect graduated from Anabuki Design College in 1994. He worked at Motokane Achitects and HAL Architects before the establishment of the studio in 2000. He defined his work as a chance to realize fresh ideas about buildings and relationships of all interactive elements. Tanijiri is also a professor at the Anabuki Design College.

the.
▶ P.018, 104 ▶ ▶ ▶

A creative collaboration between Sherwood Forlee and Mihoko Ouchi since 2009, the. is committed to produce an eclectic mix of whimsical and mirthful products without any fanciful themes or philosophies underlying their body of work.

Having started out happily as a small operation, the. is content to keep it that way. Most of the.'s products are self-funded. the. is also committed to sharing its playful spirit with not only its customers but with organizations that make positive differences in the world.

The Partners
▶ P.036-037 ▶ ▶ ▶

Named Branding Agency of the Year by Marketing Magazine and Ranked no.1 in Design Week's Creative League Table, The Partners delivers brand strategy, design and innovative ideas for clients who require outstandingly creative solutions. These include world-class brands such as Ford, Deloitte, eBay, Vodafone, the BBC, Jaguar and The National Gallery. The Partners believes that the future of business will be defined by people who think differently, not by those who think the same.

THE SMALL PRINT
▶ P.212-215 ▶ ▶ ▶

A creative agency of Richard Seabrooke and Bren Byrne founded on the idea of bringing together passionate, original minds from many disciplines, with the aim to produce unique, memorable projects and events.

Timothy Berg and Rebekah Myers
▶ P.216-221 ▶ ▶ ▶

An art collaborative based in California, the USA, the duo received their Bachelor of Fine Art degrees from the University of Colorado at Boulder. Berg received his Master of Fine Arts degree from the New York State College of Ceramics at Alfred University while Myers continued her studies in graphic design at the California College of the Arts. Berg and Myers have exhibited their work widely in the United States and in Mexico, Sweden, South Korea and Kuwait.

Torafu Architects
▶ P.108 ▶ ▶ ▶

Founded in 2004 by Koichi Suzuno and Shinya Kamuro. The duo works for a diverse range of projects, from architectural design to interior design for shops and exhibitions, product design, spatial installations and filmmaking. They have received numerous prizes including the Design for Asia (DFA) Grand Award in 2005 and the Grand Prize of the Elita Design Awards 2011.

WE Architecture
▶ P.236-239 ▶ ▶ ▶

Spanning from architecture, urban strategies, tangible design and utopian ideas, WE architecture is a young innovating architecture office based in Copenhagen, Denmark. Founded in 2009 by Marc Jay and Julie Schmidt-Nielsen, the studio name is based on the company philosophy that architecture is not the result of one person's stroke of genius but through teamwork and trans-disciplinary networks. The team strives to push innovative architecture forward to improve the condition of the world.

Yoshio, Hasegawa
▶ P.166-167 ▶ ▶ ▶

Represented by KEIKO gallery, Yoshio started to work as a faculty for the facility for the disables since 1999. His work is exhibited widely domestically and he has won several awards throughout the years such as the Second Grand Prize by Mino Washi AKARI Art Exhibition and the Kanakaku Award by Kankaku Museum, Miyagi.

Zarb Champagne
▶ P.040-043 ▶ ▶ ▶

Launched in 2009, Zarb Champagne targets the younger generation with fashionably, edgy bottles while other brands stay within their traditional philosophy.

The name Zarb derives from the French slang 'L'Argot' for 'bizarre'. To Zarb, champagne is a platform for art. Not only by what's inside the bottle but also what's outside. By combining 300 years of champagne with the creative minds of internationally acclaimed artists, Zarb stimulates senses just like art.

ZO_loft architecture & design
▶ P.121 ▶ ▶ ▶

Aims to discover and use inexpensive and sustainable technologies and materials, while analysing recovery and recycling processes, investigating in life-style and activities of the fellow human, providing easy marketing strategies and better understanding the differing consumpion needs of the populations in general, ZO_loft offers a mobile, dynamic, and flexible architecture, design and urban space by reinventing or hybridising functions, contaminating or showing an apparent functional disgregation. ZO_loft's work is exhibited worldwide and won several national and international awards such as Macef Design Award 2008 and International Idea Competition "Tra architettura e città" VI edition.

5.5 Designers
▶ P.024-027 ▶ ▶ ▶

A design studio started up in 2003 by Vincent Baranger, Jean-Sébastien Blanc, Anthony Lebossé, and Claire Renard. The team forces themselves to a conceptual rigour and a permanent questioning on what their designer status is. They stand in each of their creation for honest and accessible consumption alternatives. This type of responsible and optimistic design approach has reached, in five years time, a large panel of national and international institutions. Their clients include Nespresso, Baccarat, LaCie, Oberflex, Bernardaud, etc.

ACKNOWLEDGEMENTS

We would like to thank all the designers and companies who have involved in the production of this book. This project would not have been accomplished without their significant contribution to the compilation of this book. We would also like to express our gratitude to all the producers for their invaluable opinions and assistance throughout this entire project. The successful completion also owes a great deal to many professionals in the creative industry who have given us precious insights and comments. And to the many others whose names are not credited but have made specific input in this book, we thank you for your continuous support the whole time.

FUTURE EDITIONS

If you wish to participate in viction:ary's future projects and publications, please send your website or portfolio to submit@victionary.com